HTML3
MANUAL OF STYLE

HTML3
MANUAL OF STYLE

Larry Aronson

Ziff-Davis Press
Emeryville, California

Development Editor	Kelly Green
Copy Editor	Nicole Clausing
Technical Reviewers	Clay Shirky and Eric Berg
Project Coordinator	Madhu Prasher
Cover Illustration and Design	Regan Honda
Book Design	Gary Suen
Screen Graphics Editor	Pipi Diamond
Word Processing	Howard Blechman
Page Layout	Bruce Lundquist
Indexer	Carol Burbo

Ziff-Davis Press, ZD Press, and the Ziff-Davis Press logo are licensed to Macmillan Computer Publishing USA by Ziff-Davis Publishing Company, New York, New York.

Ziff-Davis Press imprint books are produced on a Macintosh computer system with the following applications: FrameMaker®, Microsoft® Word, QuarkXPress®, Adobe Illustrator®, Adobe Photoshop®, Adobe Streamline™, MacLink®Plus, Aldus® FreeHand™, Collage Plus™.

If you have comments or questions or would like to receive a free catalog, call or write:
Macmillan Computer Publishing USA
Ziff-Davis Press Line of Books
5903 Christie Avenue
Emeryville, CA 94608
800-688-0448

ISBN 1-56276-352-0

Manufactured in the United States of America
10 9 8 7 6 5 4 3 2 1

CONTENTS AT A GLANCE

TABLE OF CONTENTS

ACKNOWLEDGMENTS

I'd like to thank all the people who helped me write this book. Clay Shirky, who originally got me involved in this project, has my eternal gratitude. ZD Press's Suzanne Anthony, who guided the book through production; and Nicole Clausing and Madhu Prasher, who edited the manuscript, get a big thank you for their hard efforts and for being so wonderful to work with. I'd also like to thank the people who gave permission to display their works in the examples section and the many others who provided feedback and advice. A very special thank you hug goes to my best friend, Lynne Thigpen, for all her help and encouragement. Finally I'd like to acknowledge my deep debt of gratitude to the many people who continually sustain the Web by writing documentation and software tools and by participating in the World Wide Web and HTML discussion groups.

PREFACE

During the past two years a revolution has been happening over the world's communication networks. It's called the World Wide Web and its growth has been nothing less than phenomenal. Of course, no revolution comes out of nowhere and so it is with the World Wide Web. Developments—both technological and social—have prepared the way for the emergence of the Web. Computers, once confined only to those who could master the arcane mysteries of programming languages, are now part of the everyday world of business people, artists, and school children. The Internet, a set of protocols that permitted universities to exchange data, has now become the hottest trend of the nineties. The World Wide Web ties the two together, breaking the physical barriers of cyberspace to establish the foundation of a global electronic village.

The World Wide Web provides a means of accessing the resources of the Internet without requiring of the user the knowledge of how those resources are transmitted and stored. The Web's hypermedia paradigm expands the potential of the Internet and empowers both technical and nontechnical people alike with a simple, low-cost method of providing information, opinions, and art to a worldwide audience of millions. This book is about harlnessing that power. It is a lean 'n' mean instructional guide to HTML, the Hypertext Markup Language that is the lingua franca of the Web. In this slim volume lie the means by which you can join the revolution; to be not just a passive consumer of information, but a publisher.

This book is primarily for those who are already exploring the Web with programs such as NASA Mosaic and Netscape Navigator, and who now wish to put their own information out there for others to utilize. Don't fret if you're not there yet. Web browsers are available for most computer platforms and, in many cases, are free. Getting an Internet connection used to be rather difficult. Now, however, on the same bookshelf where this book can be found, you will find all-in-one kits that will get you connected to the Internet and have you surfing the Web in a matter of hours. HTML is very easy to learn. You do not need any prior experience with programming languages. A familiarity with any modern word processing program will suffice. Since the World Wide Web encompasses most of the other protocols of the Internet, some knowledge of basic Internet procedures, such as e-mail, FTP, gopher, and newsgroups will be helpful. Such knowledge, however, is not required to understand how the Web works and how to publish information on it.

This is a book in the middle. The first edition was written just before HTML2 was finalized. Today, HTML is in the middle of the transition to level 3. The Web itself is moving from an academic to a commercial focus, and yours truly is in the middle of a career change from programmer/analyst to author/lecturer. Some of the topics covered herein are illustrated using products that were still in beta testing, which means that my best guess today may not accurately describe where the Web will be tomorrow. This book will get you started in Web publishing; the rest of your education will come online.

The remainder of this book consists of seven chapters and an appendix with a quick reference to HTML and a resource guide. Chapter 1 provides an introduction to HTML, the basic concepts of hypertext and hypermedia, the World Wide Web and the Internet. Chapter 2 explains the structure and syntax of the language and covers the details of the various elements. Chapter 3 provides a discussion of proper HTML style and shows how to avoid common mistakes. Chapter 4 is a tutorial-style walk through of three typical Web applications. Chapter 5 covers some advanced design techniques and Chapter 6 provides an overview of what can be done with a Web server. Finally, Chapter 7 presents a collection of World Wide Web pages and the complete HTML source that generates each example page. If you are one of those people who has to try something out before you understand it, turn to the second example in Chapter 7 for a quick start to creating a World Wide Web home page.

This book was created and edited on my Apple Macintosh 7100/80 and PowerBook 160 computers using Microsoft Word version 5.1. Additional research was done on my nameless Pentium computer running Linux, a public domain version of the UNIX operating system. Manuscript pages were printed on an Apple Personal LaserWriter NTR printer. Several World Wide Web browsers were used—primarily Netscape Navigator, but also NCSA Mosaic and Arena, the HTML3 test bed browser from the World Wide Web Consortium. My connection to the Internet is via a dial-up PPP (Point-to-Point Protocol) link to Interport Communications, a local Internet service provider, using a US Robotics V.34 modem.

This revised edition was written while much of HTML and the World Wide Web was in flux. I welcome your comments, suggestions, and criticism. Please send them via e-mail to: laronson@acm.org. Thanks, and enjoy.

—**Larry Aronson**
New York City

What Is HTML?

HTML: A STANDARD GENERALIZED
   MARKUP LANGUAGE

HYPERTEXT AND HYPERMEDIA

MOSAIC, THE WORLD WIDE WEB, AND
   THE INTERNET

Chapter

1

Hypertext Markup Language (HTML) is a system for marking up documents with tags that indicate how text in the documents should be presented and how the documents are linked together. Hypertext links are quite powerful. Within the HTML markup scheme lies the power to create interactive, cross-platform, multimedia, client-server applications. This string of adjectives is not just hype; such systems do exist. One, called the World Wide Web (also known as WWW or just simply, The Web), lives on the Internet, providing organization to a wide variety of computer resources located around the globe.

The Web is an interlinked collection of living documents containing formatted text, images, and sound. These documents are organized into webspaces. A webspace is typically structured around a home page with links to other pages or documents both in and outside of the webspace. A home page functions as a virtual meeting place in cyberspace for the exchange of information. Creating a home page is easy. You write it in HTML.

To make it even easier, there are many home pages with information about HTML and the World Wide Web. HTML is a language under construction. The continuing development of HTML is conducted on the Web in an open process that you can be part of. New tools and techniques appear frequently and are quickly spread throughout the community of Web authors.

HTML: A STANDARD GENERALIZED MARKUP LANGUAGE

HTML is not a programming language and an HTML document is not a computer program. It's a lot simpler than that. A computer program is a series of procedures and instructions applied, typically, to external data. An HTML document, however, *is* the data. The definition of HTML specifies the grammar and syntax of markup tags that, when inserted into the data, instruct browsers—computer programs that read HTML documents—how to present the document.

In traditional publishing, the author supplies content in the form of a manuscript which an editor marks up with instructions for the printer specifying the layout and typography of the work. The printer, following the markup, typesets the pages and reproduces copies for distribution. With the Web and HTML, you are both the author and the editor, and your work is a set of files on a Web server. A single marked-up version of each page is "visited" by your readers, not distributed to them. The page is typeset by each reader's browser with layout and typography appropriate to the browser's computer environment and the reader's preferences.

Technically, HTML is defined as a Standard Generalized Markup Language (SGML) Document Type Definition (DTD). An HTML document is said to be an *instance* of an SGML document.

SGML originated as GML (General Markup Language) at IBM in the late 1960s as an attempt to solve some of the problems of transporting documents across different computer systems. The term *markup* comes from the publishing industry. SGML is generalized, meaning that instead of specifying exactly how to present a document, it describes document types, along with markup languages to format and present instances of each type. GML became SGML when it was accepted as a standard by the International Standards Organization (ISO) in Geneva, Switzerland (reference number ISO 8879:1986).

An SGML document has three parts. The first describes the character set and, most importantly, which characters are used to differentiate the text from the markup tags. The second part declares the document type and which markup tags are accepted as legal. The third part is called the document instance and contains the actual text and the markup tags. The three parts need not be in the same physical file, which is a good thing because it allows us to forget about SGML and deal only with HTML. All HTML browsers assume the same information for the SGML character-set and document-type declarations, so we only have to work with HTML document instances—simple text files.

The base character set of an HTML document is Latin-1 (ISO 8859/1). It's an 8-bit alphabet with characters for most American and European languages. Plain old ASCII (ISO 646) is a 7-bit subset of Latin-1. There is no obligation to use anything but the 128 standard ASCII characters in an HTML document. In fact, sticking to straight ASCII is encouraged as it allows an HTML document to be edited by any text editor on any computer system and be transported over any network by even the most rudimentary of e-mail and data transport systems. To make this possible, HTML includes character entities for most of the commonly used non-ASCII Latin-1 characters. These character entities begin with the ampersand character (&), followed by the name or number of the character, followed by a semicolon. For example, the character entity for a small *e* with a grave accent (`) is è.

HTML markup tags are delimited by the angle brackets, < and >. They appear either singularly, like the tag <P> to indicate a paragraph break in the text, or as a pair of starting and ending tags that modify the content contained. <B>Attention!</B>, for example, is an instruction to present the text string Attention! in a bold typeface. There are tags for formatting text, tags for specifying hypertext links, tags for including sound and picture elements, and tags for defining input fields for interactive pages.

That's all there is to Hypertext Markup Language—character entities and markup tags. However, this system of entities and tags is evolving. There are currently several standardization levels of HTML.

Level 1 is the level mandatory for all WWW browsers. It is essentially what was accepted by the first browsers (level 0), plus images.

Level 2 includes all the elements of level 1, plus tags for defining user input fields. This is currently the standard although many browsers already support level 3 elements.

Level 3, also known as HTML 3, is being finalized. It includes markup tags for objects such as tables, figures, and mathematical equations.

The next chapter describes the HTML language, including most level 3 features. Almost all of the development work on HTML is done on the Internet in the form of discussion groups, which post proposed changes and issue requests for comments. The complete specifications of HTML (the SGML DTD) can always be found on the Web. The Web is also the place to look for the most up-to-date HTML and SGML documentation, most of it in hypertext. Appendix B has a listing of Web addresses for many of these documents.

Hypertext and hypermedia

Hypertext is text that is not constrained to be linear. In reading this book, for example, you may skip some chapters and make occasional trips to the appendices. Still, it is, as presented to you, a linear sequence of pages. In contrast, hypertext organizes information as an interconnected web of linked text. Different paths can be followed through the work by different readers; readers can choose, among all the links the authors provided, those associations most relevant to their immediate needs.

Hypermedia refers to hypertext applications that contain things other than text objects. Hypermedia applications encompass images, video, sound, and more. The Hypertext Markup Language contains markup tags for specifying links to multimedia objects. How these objects are displayed is left up to the browser, but generally, images are expanded as illustrations or figures within the text, while sound and animation are presented in their own windows with stop and play controls.

Links from an HTML hypertext page appear as highlighted text, usually blue and underlined. The text itself is called the anchor of the link and can be embedded in other HTML elements, like lists and tables. Images can be anchors as well as text. Small images can be used as clickable icons. This is useful for creating navigational controls that appear on a series of Web pages. Images can also have defined sub-areas; each an anchor linking to somewhere else. Such images are called *imagemaps* and are quite handy for organizing spatially related data.

The wonderful thing about hypertext is that it adds an extra dimension of structure to the content of your work. With hypertext, you can highlight alternative relationships in the text besides the linear ordering of sections, chapters, and subchapters found in the table of contents. The size of a hypertext work is limited only by the physical storage space available. Since the World Wide Web is on and of the Internet, this means that terabytes of data are organized and given structure by the Web. Because it's growing faster than any one person could possibly keep up with, your experience is that of "surfing" through an unbounded information space.

The concepts of hypertext and hypermedia have been around for a while; Ted Nelson is given credit for coining the terms in 1965. One of the first practical hypermedia applications was the Aspen Movie Map done at MIT in 1978. It used videodisc and touch-screen technology. Filevision from Telos, released in 1984, gave hypermedia databases to early Macintosh users. In 1987, Apple introduced Hypercard, written by Bill Atkinson, which incorporated many hypermedia concepts. Windows users take advantage of a hypertext based help system. The development of CD-ROM drives for personal computers made the commercial development and marketing of multimedia applications a reality. And in 1989, Tim Berners-Lee and Robert Cailliau submitted a proposal to their colleagues at CERN for a client-server-based hypermedia system, and the World Wide Web was born.

HTML hypermedia applications are similar in many ways to Macintosh Hypercard applications; enough so that it's possible to mimic simple Hypercard applications in HTML and vice versa. Both systems take the form of a web of linked nodes with one node designated as home—the home stack for Hypercard and the home page for a Web server. The differences, however, are significant; not the least important of which is that Hypercard applications only run on Apple Macintosh computers, whereas HTML applications run on networks connecting a variety of computers.

Unlike a Hypercard card, an HTML page can be many physical pages long, corresponding to a chapter in a book or a section of a manual; however, the width is variable—the browser presenting the page word-wraps the text and positions the images to fit the width of the display window. HTML hypertext links are activated by clicking with a mouse button on highlighted text or image. The link may be to a point in the text on the same page, to a new Web page, or to some other object or resource on the network.

Another key difference between other hypermedia and HTML/Web applications is that the former are designed for running on individual personal computers—every user has their own copy. HTML documents, on the other hand, exist in a client/server environment where one copy serves all. The clients are the readers' browsers. The servers are programs running on remote computers that provide the Web pages requested by the browsers. Because media (paper and plastic) doesn't have to be physically reproduced and distributed each time information is added or changed, Web pages can be updated quickly at low cost.

The next section will have more to say about browsers. A full discussion of servers, however, is beyond the scope of this book. Suffice it to say that most but not all Web servers are running on UNIX machines with high-speed connections to the Internet.

For an HTML application to be "on the Web" means that the HTML files and other documents that make up the application must reside in a directory that is accessible to a server. Usually a Web server, however, non-interactive HTML files can reside on ftp or gopher servers, too. Note that this does not mean there must be a link from some existing Web page to your document in order for your document to be part of the Web. There is a unique address, called a Uniform Resource Locator (URL), for practically every file and resource on the Internet. There are URL formats for resources such as Gophers,

Wide Area Information Servers (WAIS), ftp archives, and USENET news-groups. Since most browsers have the ability to load any URL entered by the user, just about anything on the Internet is also on the World Wide Web.

MOSAIC, THE WORLD WIDE WEB, AND THE INTERNET

A lot has been written recently about the World Wide Web. What's all the excitement about? Are Web browsers the "killer apps" of the 1990s? My guess is that they are. The first time you start exploring the Web with a graphical browser like Mosaic or Netscape, you have the astonishing sensation of a myth turning into reality before your eyes. The myth is the dream of a universal information repository that science fiction writers have given us over the past half-century. Today, with our browsers and the Web, we indeed have a simple, easy-to-use interface for all the computerized information in the world.

Mosaic was the first graphical browser for the Web. There are now many. An up-to-date listing of browsers and related software is usually available from a link on the Web home page, http://www.w3.org/hypertext/WWW/Clients.html. Mosaic was written by graduate students at the National Center for Super computing Activities (NCSA) at the University of Illinois in Urbana, home of the HAL 9000. Many other browsers are built on Mosaic technology licensed from the U of I. Mosaic is available in versions for Macintosh, Windows, and UNIX/X-Windows systems, and it's free.

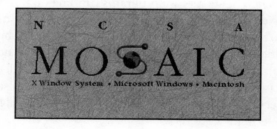

Some of the graduate students that created Mosaic left to form a new company, now called Netscape Communications. Their browser, Netscape Navigator, features extensions to HTML that provide greater artistic freedom to the Web author. It has become the most popular browser, by far. Like Mosaic, it comes in versions for Macintosh, Windows, and UNIX/X-Windows systems. It's free for nonprofit and educational use.

Although hyped as the cutting edge of technology, Web browsers are really very simple programs based on technology that has been around for a while. They've achieved their impact by taking advantage of today's sophisticated computer networks and operating systems to do stuff that people want to do better and cheaper, that's all.

This book uses the current Macintosh version of Netscape Navigator for screen shots and examples of formatted HTML documents. The results will look much the same for Netscape's Windows and UNIX versions using the default preferences. The examples should also produce similar results for other graphical browsers like Mosaic or Prodigy's Web browser. The images used in this chapter are from the NCSA Mosaic home page at http://www.ncsa.uiuc.edu/SDG/Software/Mosaic/Docs/help-about.html, The World Wide Web Consortium's home page at http://www.w3.org/, and from a Visualization study of the Internet at http://www.ncsa.uiuc.edu/SCMS/DigLib/text/technology/Visualization-Study-NSFNET-Cox.html.

There are three ways you can browse the Web: in TTY or linemode, through a commercial online service provider, or as an Internet host.

Linemode browsers are level 1 browsers that display text in a single font. They connect to the Web via Telnet and dial-up BBSs. Probably the most popular of these is Lynx from the University of Kansas, which works with DEC VT-100s, a common display terminal that's emulated by most telecommunications software. Cursor keys are used instead of a mouse to select and activate links.

The big commercial online service providers, such as CompuServe, America Online, and Prodigy have graphical Web browsing capabilities in their software. They differ in pricing and capability and in what support they provide for authors who wish to publish on the Web. Still, the online services provide the easiest ways to get wired.

The third and best way is to have your computer directly connected to the Internet using TCP/IP—the transport protocol of the Internet. You can connect via a local area network that has a gateway to the Internet, or you can connect to an Internet service provider with a dial-up or cable modem. This kind of setup is the most complicated technically, but, for heavy use, it is much more economical; many Internet service providers charge flat monthly fees for unlimited connect time.

Most browsers can access documents locally—in other words, you can implement an HTML application on your own computer or local area network and not be connected to the Internet at all. For your application to be part of the World Wide Web, however, your documents must be on the Internet. You can run your own server if you have a direct Internet connection (and your system administrator's approval). There is free server software from CERN, NCSA, and others. Generally though, it's better to find space on someone else's Web server and rely on their expertise to keep their machine and your webspace available 24 hours a day.

World Wide Web Initiative

Is the World Wide Web the same thing as the Internet? Well, yes and no. The Internet is physically much bigger than the Web, yet just about everything on the Internet can be accessed by a link from a Web page, so in a way, the Web is the Internet seen from a different point of view—one not tied down to the physical hardware.

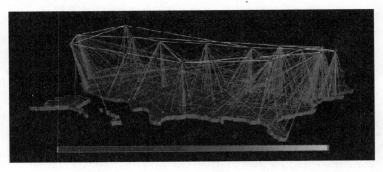

The Internet started in the late 1960s as a U.S. Department of Defense experiment to see if the nation's university and military research computers could be linked in a way that would survive a nuclear attack. The design called for a network without hierarchy or center—each computer on the Internet is the equal of any other.

More and more institutions joined their networks to the Internet in the 1970s and people started using it for their own purposes, like exchanging e-mail and hosting science fiction discussion groups. In the early 1980s, the military bailed out and got their own network. The National Science Foundation took over responsibility for the government's hardware, which it has since transferred to private hands. Still, no one owns or runs the Internet. It is a cooperative community of people using computer networks to exchange information.

In the last few years, Internet growth has been explosive. Thousands of new users are connecting to it every day. Hundreds of new Internet service providers have come into business, offering the public low-cost connections. A design that permitted no centers of authority has become the largest functioning anarchy in the world. Now, the World Wide Web is here; it's the ideal way to organize the Internet's diverse resources. It's time to learn HTML.

The HTML Language

Overview

Structure tags

Styles

Anchors and links

Inline images

Forms

Chapter 2

This chapter presents the various elements of the HTML language—
the syntax of character entities and markup tags, and how they are interpreted by a browser to display a page. This description corresponds
to the HTML 2.0 standard extended with features proposed for the HTML 3.0
standard by the World Wide Web Consortium's HTML Working Group,
Netscape Communications Corporation, Spry Incorporated, and others. While
it is not practical to address all the possible directions the language may take,
the material that is provided here is sufficient for presenting your information
in a professional and attractive manner.

OVERVIEW

A page on the World Wide Web is composed of a set of files stored somewhere
on some device that's accessible to a Web server, or, at the very least, an ftp
server. The exact somewhere of a page is known by its URL (Uniform Resource
Locator). A Web page has content consisting of text and inline images. The
page's marked up text is in one file and each individual image is in a separate
file. Images are typically referenced by their filenames so the same image can
be used more than once on a page or on many different pages. All other multimedia is accessed through helper applications or players that are launched by
the browser when the reader clicks on a link. The documentation or online
help for your browser will list the recommended helper applications appropriate to your operating system.

Authoring Web pages is different in many respects from traditional desktop
publishing. For one thing, a page has no fixed size. The reader's browser will

word-wrap the text to fit the width of the display window and enable scrolling to accommodate the length. In desktop publishing, you specify fonts, type styles and sizes, and the precise placement of text and images. As a Web author, you have only general control over the typography and layout of your page.

What you do when you write a Web page is insert markup tags that describe the elements of the page in an abstract language that's not dependent on the properties of any display device. After all, you don't know what fonts are available on your readers' computers or how their browsers are configured. After you upload the marked up file to a Web server, you're done. The actual typography and layout of the page is the responsibility of the reader's browser.

The advantages of this approach are obvious. Having one electronic copy of your work that can serve all your readers is more efficient than pushing tons of paper and ink around the world. Pages on the World Wide Web can be updated with new information more quickly and cheaply than paper pages.

The point is that Web pages are living documents, requiring continuing care and maintenance. Webspaces, in particular, have the tendency to grow like weeds. Existing pages are cloned and adapted to new uses continually. Unlike traditional desktop publishing pages, which are finished works rushed out the door to meet a deadline, Web pages are perpetually "under construction."

PAGE STRUCTURE

A file containing the marked up text of a Web page is called an HTML file. It begins and ends with the tags <HTML> and </HTML>. It is divided into two parts, a head and a body. The head contains information about the document and the body contains the text of the document. Markup tags are used to define the two parts, as in this minimal HTML file:

```
<HTML>
<HEAD>
<TITLE>Minimal HTML Page</TITLE>
</HEAD>
<BODY>

Your text goes here with embedded HTML markup tags that
describe the elements of the page and specify where the inline
images go. Browsers automatically remove redundant white space
from a paragraph and word-wrap the text to fit the width of the
browser's display window.

</BODY>
</HTML>
```

It's important to understand that it is the markup elements <HEAD></HEAD> and <BODY></BODY> that divide the page into its two parts and not the carriage returns and line spacing used. If all carriage returns were removed from the above example and replaced with blanks, it would still generate the same page. In this example, the head contains the title of the page and the body contains a paragraph of text word-wrapped to fit the browser window. As noted in the example text, all extra white space—carriage returns, linefeeds, tabs, control characters, and redundant blanks—are removed. You are free to use these characters to improve the readability of your HTML files without affecting the rendering of the page in a Web browser.

In the above example, the only information specified in the head of the document is the document's title. For most pages, this is all you will find in the document's head. Certain other informational tags can go there, including style sheet declarations. Most other head tags represent advanced features that may or may not be supported by your Web server. Check with your systems administrator or your local webmaster to find out what features are supported by your web server software.

Every page should have a title—preferably a short one that's meaningful in the larger context of the work. With most browsers, the title appears either as the title of the display window or at the top of that window. Titles are not absolutely required; many text documents on the Web are simply text files, containing no markup elements and having no titles. Most browsers are quite forgiving and will accept the page with or without a title. Most will allow you to omit the head and body tags, although it's a good idea to keep them in. The opening BODY tag, for instance, is where you can specify page background and text colors other than the browser's defaults. See Chapter 5 for more information on how to do this.

HTML ELEMENTS

There are only a few general syntax rules to learn in HTML. First, there are two kinds of HTML elements; markup tags and character entities. The minimal HTML page above contains three markup tags. A character entity is an escape sequence that defines a single character that cannot normally be entered in the text content. A character entity begins with an ampersand (&) and is followed by either the name of a predefined entity or a pound sign (#) followed by the decimal number of the character, as defined in the ISO Latin-1 character set, included in Appendix A. A semicolon is used to terminate the character entity. The tilde (~), for example, can be generated by the sequence ~.

Character entities are predefined for characters from the ISO Latin-1 alphabet that are not defined in ASCII, and characters that are needed to mark the beginnings and ends of HTML elements. A complete list of predefined character entities can be found in Appendix A. Three are particularly useful as they are the entities that must be used if you want to show a character that would ordinarily be taken as the beginning (or end) of a character entity or markup tag:

&lt;	"<"	The left-angle bracket or less-than sign
&gt;	">"	The right-angle bracket or greater-than sign
&amp;	"&"	The ampersand

Also useful are

&quot;	"''"	The double quote mark
	" "	A nonbreaking space
&copy;	"©"	The copyright symbol

TAG SYNTAX

Every markup tag has a tag ID (or name) and possibly some attributes. Markup tags are either empty or nonempty. Nonempty tags, also called containers, act upon text enclosed in a pair of starting and ending tags. A starting tag begins with the left angle bracket (<) followed immediately by the tag ID, zero or more attributes separated by spaces, then the right angle bracket (>) to close the tag. Ending tags are exactly the same except that there is a slash (/) immediately between the opening left angle bracket and the tag ID. Ending tags do not contain attributes. Whereas containers modify content, empty tags insert things into the content. The empty tag stands alone; there's no corresponding ending tag with a slash. Here are some examples of empty tags:

 Line break, following text begins at the left margin.
<HR> Horizontal rule, draw a line across the page.

The following empty tag specifies that an inline image be inserted. It has one attribute, the SRC attribute, whose value is the name (source) of the file containing the image:

```
<IMG SRC="corplogo.gif">
```

Attributes take the form of NAME=VALUE, where the value is appropriate to the domain of the attribute. The value should be enclosed in double quotes, although it's safe to drop the quotes when the value is a simple number or constant. If there's more than one attribute in a tag, they are separated by blanks, not commas. Some attributes are specified just by the name, for example, BORDER is equivalent to BORDER="yes", which is also the same as BORDER=1.

Here are some examples of nonempty tags:

```
<TITLE>Don Quixote's Home Page</TITLE>
<I>This should appear in italics</I>
<TT>Fixed width, typewriter font</TT>
<A HREF="catalog.html">our current catalog</A>
```

The last example above is an anchor. Anchors are tags that define the nodes of hypertext links. In this example, the phrase "our current catalog" will be highlighted by the browser (usually by making it blue and underlined) to indicate that clicking on it (or selecting it if you're using a nongraphical browser) will link the reader to another page, in this case, the file *catalog.html*—the value of the HREF (Hypertext REFerence) attribute. (See "Anchors and Links" later in this chapter for more on addressing formats.)

Here's a simple example illustrating the use of markup tags and character entities:

```
<HEAD>
<TITLE>Simple HTML Example</TITLE>
</HEAD>
<BODY>
<H1>Level 1 Headings</H1>
<P>Whereas <STRONG>Titles</STRONG> should have some relation to the
outside world, Level 1 Headings should introduce the major sections of
the work.</P> <P>This is a second paragraph of text inserted to show
how paragraph tags are used to separate text and to point out the use
of the &lt;STRONG&gt; tag in the first paragraph.</P>
</BODY>
```

Figure 2.1 shows what this example looks like on a Macintosh using Netscape with the default preferences set.

First, note that the title of the page, Simple HTML Example, appears in the window title. The body of this example page consists of a level 1 heading marked with the <H1> and </H1> tags, and two paragraphs of text enclosed by paragraph tags, <P> and </P>. You can also see how Mosaic has ignored the carriage returns placed in the HTML page and word-wrapped the text to fit the width of its window.

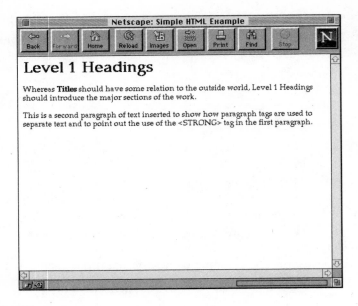

Figure 2.1: Markup tags

In the second paragraph, in order to get the string <STRONG> to appear without being interpreted as a tag, character entities are used—< for the less-than sign (<), and > for the greater-than sign (>).

Although the HTML text in this example is neatly formatted, it doesn't actually matter where the tags are placed with respect to the page. The following HTML segments will all produce the exact same heading as Figure 2.1:

```
<H1>Level 1 Headings</H1>
<h1>
Level 1 Headings
</h1>
<H1>Level 1
Headings</h1 >
```

That's right! Tag elements are not case sensitive. You can freely mix upper- and lowercase letters. Spaces are only allowed after the tag ID and before the closing bracket, though there's little reason to put any there. The string

```
< H1 >What Went Wrong?< /H1 >
```

will not be processed as a heading. The brackets and their contents will be ignored and only the enclosed text, What Went Wrong? (which is *not*, by the way, what WWW stands for!), will appear. Browsers are very tolerant of errors; most are just ignored. If an anchor tag is correct but the link is in error, then browsers will return a status message such as "Unable to connect to remote host" or "Unable to access document."

Markup tags usually can be nested—for example, anchors inside of list structures. However, some nestings are not allowed—for example, anchors inside of other anchors or a heading inside preformatted text. Other nestings are allowed but discouraged—for example, using style tags inside a heading.

You can place comments in an HTML document to annotate your work just as you would with other computer languages. Comments are completely ignored by the browser. An HTML comment is actually an SGML comment. It starts with the string <!--, can contain any character, and ends with the first occurrence of the string -->. As a general rule, place each comment on a separate line and avoid using any of the special characters, like <, >, &, or !. Some older browsers may not parse the comment correctly. Comments cannot be nested.

STRUCTURE TAGS

HTML tags can be divided into two loose classes—those that change the page structure and those that change text styles. Into the structure class go tags for designating headings, paragraphs, lists, and tables. Structure tags always imply paragraph breaks before and after the marked-up text and, thus, create the layout of the page. Style tags affect the typography of the text—font size and styles—but do not modify the layout. The anchor tag, which creates a link, falls into the style class, since its only visual effect is to highlight the text that anchors the link. Image and figure tags are in a class all their own and will be discussed later on in this chapter.

HEADINGS

Major divisions of a document are introduced and separated by headings. HTML supports six levels of headings, designated by the tag pairs <H1></H1>, <H2></H2>, <H3></H3>, <H4></H4>, <H5></H5>, and <H6></H6>. This is sufficient for most hypertext applications, because much of the structure of a hypertext work is in the web of links. Additional structure can be generated by using list and table elements. All heading tags are containers and require a corresponding end tag.

H1 is the highest level of heading. It is customary to put a level 1 heading as the first element in the body of the home page to serve as the internal title of the page, as opposed to the window title which is created by the <TITLE></TITLE>

tags. A heading element implies a style change, including a paragraph break before and after the heading, and whatever white space is needed to render a heading of that level. Adding style tags to a heading or inserting paragraph tags to emphasize the heading is neither required nor recommended.

Headings should be used in their natural hierarchical order, as in an outline although it is legal to skip heading levels—to follow an H1 with an H3, for example. Here is an HTML page illustrating the six different heading levels:

```
<HEAD>
<TITLE>Heading Levels</TITLE>
</HEAD>
<BODY>
<H1>Level 1 Heading</H1>
First paragraph of text.
<H2>Level 2 Heading</H2>
Second paragraph of text.
<H3>Level 3 Heading</H3>
Third paragraph of text.
<H4>Level 4 Heading</H4>
Fourth paragraph of text.
<H5>Level 5 Heading</H5>
Fifth paragraph of text.
<H6>Level 6 Heading</H6>
Sixth paragraph of text.
</BODY>
```

Figure 2.2 shows how these headings will appear.

By default, headings are aligned to the left margin. By adding the ALIGN attribute to the tag, other alignments can be achieved. Figure 2.3, generated by the following HTML, shows how a set of centered headings can create a playbill effect.

```
<H3 ALIGN=center>HTML Manual of Style</H3>
<H5 ALIGN=center>presents</H5>
<H1 ALIGN=center>A Centered Heading</H1>
<H5 ALIGN=center>fig. 2.3</H5>
```

Like tag names, attribute names are not case sensitive. My convention is to use uppercase for tag and attribute names and lowercase for attribute values (except for URLs, which should always be considered case sensitive). You're free to adopt any other convention, or abandon all convention entirely.

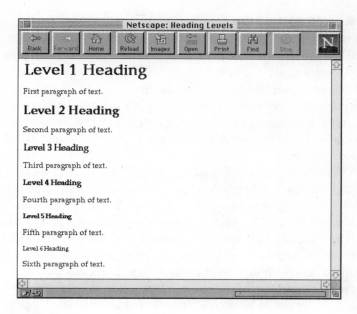

Figure 2.2: Headings

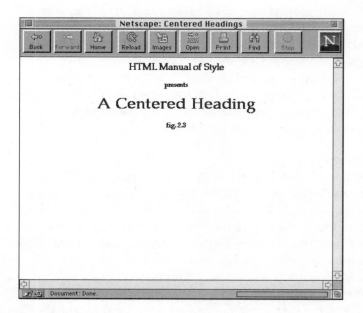

Figure 2.3: Centered headings

COMMON ATTRIBUTES

ALIGN is one of a set of common attributes that can be used with headings and most of the other structural markup tags described in this chapter.

The ALIGN attribute can have the values, "left" (the default), "center", "right", and "justify". Some other browsers recognize the <CENTER></CENTER> tags for the positioning of page elements. This is a Netscape extension and the general feeling at the time of this writing is that it won't be included in the final specification for HTML3 but will remain as an extension to HTML recognized by most popular browsers.

NOWRAP can be specified (equivalent to NOWRAP="yes") with most tags to turn off normal text wrapping. Within the text contained by the tags, line breaks (<BR>) must be used to separate the lines. There's also a Netscape extension, the <NOBR></NOBR> tags, that does much the same thing.

The ID attribute can be added to a tag to assign a name to the enclosed content. This name can then be specified as part of an URL thus providing the ability to link to specific points within the body of a document. There's more on this in the section on anchors and links later on in this chapter.

The LANG attribute can be used to specify that an alternate language should be applied to the tags content. This affects hyphenation rules and the choice of ligatures and quotation marks.

The CLASS attribute is used to assign a class name to the content of the HTML element. Class names are referenced in style sheets for more precise typographic control. The value of the CLASS attribute is a simple name. See Chapter 5 for more about style sheets.

The CLEAR attribute is used in conjunction with content that flows around images and figures. It is an instruction to space down the page, as far as necessary, until the margin is clear before placing the content. The CLEAR attribute can have a value of "left", "right", or "all".

PARAGRAPHS

Paragraphs are referred to in HTML as block elements and include plain text paragraphs and some special purpose paragraphs, such as external quotes, side notes, footers, and such. Browsers insert paragraph breaks and extra line spacing before and after all block elements. In the text contained within a block element, all carriage returns, tabs, control characters, and redundant blanks are replaced with single spaces and the text is word-wrapped to fit the reader's display window.

Your everyday plain text paragraph is created by paragraph tags, <P></P>. The first line of the paragraph may or may not appear indented—that's up to the browser. The paragraph is the simplest HTML page element and may

contain any of the common attributes mentioned above. For example, to center a paragraph of text, you would code:

```
<P ALIGN=center>Just a few words here</P>.
```

In HTML2, the paragraph tag was an empty tag, without attributes, that
forced text, that would normally flow together, into two separate paragraphs.
In HTML3 the paragraph tag is a container and separates a block of text from
other page elements. It's a small but significant change. In HTML2, content is
marked up only if it must be treated differently from plain text. In HTML3 all
content is marked up. From the language developers' point of view, having
plain paragraphs belong to a broader class of objects called block elements
makes the HTML cleaner to implement. The HTML2 approach seems the
more natural style for pages where most of the content is straight paragraphs
of text, but the HTML3 approach is much better when the paragraphs need attributes and are intermixed with other elements. Since most browsers are back-
wardly compatible with pages written for HTML2, both approaches will work;
however, HTML editors that do syntax checking may issue a warning or error
message on finding an HTML2-style empty paragraph tag.

When all you need to do is end the current line and have the next one begin
at the margin, use the line break tag, <BR>. It is an empty tag, differing from
the paragraph tag in that it does not insert any extra white space. You can think
of it as inserting a newline character into the text. Line break tags should be
used where more than one line is needed in a heading or list item.

HTML provides a horizontal rule element for visually organizing headings
and paragraphs into larger units. The horizontal rule tag, <HR> (an empty
tag), instructs the reader's browser to insert a paragraph break into the content
with a line separating the paragraphs. It's a nice feature, as the browser will adjust the line to fit the width of the display window.

A couple of things can be done with the horizontal rule. Netscape Navigator
recognizes additional attributes to this tag. The SIZE attribute specifies the
height of the rule in pixels and the WIDTH attribute specifies its horizontal
extent. With the specification of a WIDTH attribute, ALIGN is meaningful.
For example:

```
<HR SIZE=4 WIDTH=50% ALIGN=center>
```

specifies a horizontal rule four pixels tall, aligned in the center of the window,
occupying exactly half of the display width.

The following example has a heading, paragraphs, line breaks, and horizontal rules.

```
<HEAD>
<TITLE>Paragraphs and Line Breaks</TITLE>
</HEAD>
<BODY>
<H1>Twelve</H1>
<HR>
<P>The five colors blind the eye.<BR>
The five tones deafen the ear.<BR>
The five flavors dull the taste.<BR>
Racing and hunting madden the mind.<BR>
Precious things lead one astray.</P>
<P>Therefore the sage is guided by what
he feels and not by what he sees.<BR>
He lets go of that and chooses this.</P>
<HR>
</BODY>
```

Figure 2.4 shows this example.

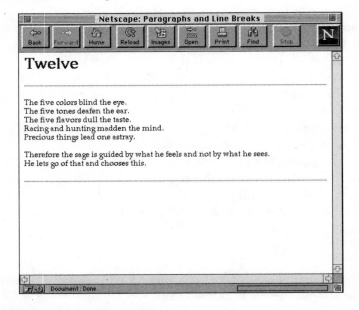

Figure 2.4: Paragraphs and line breaks

BLOCK ELEMENTS

Often some portion of a page's content is material quoted from an external work. To visually distinguish such paragraphs, the blockquote element is used. The tags are written <BLOCKQUOTE></BLOCKQUOTE> and contained text is rendered as a paragraph within wider right and left margins than a plain text paragraph (see Figure 2.5 below). If more than one paragraph is quoted, it's permissible to use empty paragraph tags to separate the paragraphs within the blockquote rather than using separate blockquote tags to enclose each paragraph.

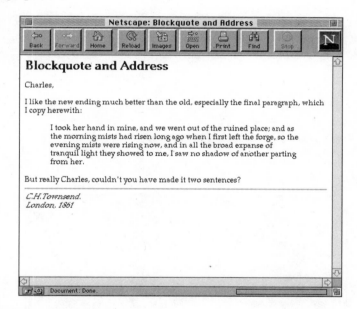

Figure 2.5: Blockquote and address

The address element, written <ADDRESS></ADDRESS>, is used for signatures, addresses, and other authorship information usually appearing at the top or bottom of a page. Address text is typically rendered in italic and may be indented or right justified. No more than a single paragraph of text should be in an address block. Use line break tags, <BR>, if you want to layout the address content as separate lines of information.

The note element, written <NOTE></NOTE>, is used for side notes and other extra text material. Notes are typically indented or boxed or rendered in a smaller type size, often with an accompanying icon to visually indicate the role of the note with respect to the main text. The role is determined by the value of the ROLE attribute. Figure 2.6, generated by the following HTML, shows a note element use as a "tip."

```
<H1> Here's a good tip </H1>
<HR>
<NOTE ROLE=tip>
It's useful to keep a low end browser around, such as an early version
of Mosaic, as a check that your pages will look good with any browser.
</NOTE>
<HR>

<P>If no ROLE value is specified no icon should be generated. On the
other hand, the SRC attribute can be used to specify a custom icon, as
in:</P>

<HR>
<NOTE ROLE=warning SRC="warn.gif">
MAKE SURE THE POWER IS OFF!<BR> BEFORE REMOVING THE COVER
</NOTE>
<HR>
```

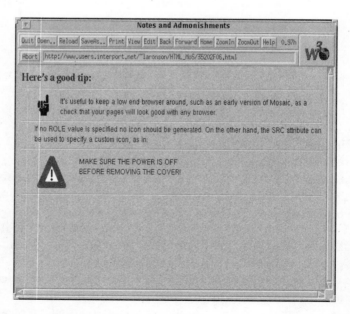

Figure 2.6: Notes and Admonishments

Like the address element, notes are intended for single paragraphs of text.

Footnotes are handled somewhat differently since there's no physical foot to a Web page. The content of the footnote is contained in the tags, <FN></FN>, and is displayed (typically in a popup window) when the reader clicks on a reference to the footnote. Within the text, the reference to the footnote is created by the anchor tag with the ID attribute to link the two together. This gives you some freedom in styling the footnote. Here's a segment of HTML with two footnotes. The reference to the first footnote is a standard looking hypertext link. The reference to the second uses a superscripted asterisk.

```
<P>It's a wonder that anyone takes on the responsibility of a large
computer project. The inherent problems, so well documented by <A
HREF="#fn1">Frederick Brooks</A>, can seem overwhelming. Yet, there's
always room for optimism. Recent research<A HREF="#fn2"><SUP>*</SUP></A>
has demonstrated that Murphy's Law is only 88% correct.</P>
<FN ID="fn1"><CITE>The Mythical Man-Month</CITE> by Frederick P. Brooks,
Addison Wesley, 1975. A series of essays, drawn from the author's
experience as project manager for the IBM System 360 Computer and the
OS/360 operating system.</FN>

<FN ID="fn2"><CITE>A Probabilistic Formulation of Murphy Dynamics as
Applied to the Analysis of Operational Research Problems</CITE> by
William R. Simpson, The Journal of Irreproducible Results, 1983.</FN>
```

The banner element, <BANNER></BANNER>, is used to fix a block of text to a position relative to the display window, rather than the page. Banner text remains in its position as the rest of the page's content scrolls underneath.

The preformatted text block element is sort of an antiparagraph. Any text between the starting and ending tags, <PRE></PRE>, will be left essentially as it is—well, almost, anyway. Preformatted text is rendered in a monospaced font, and all line breaks and redundant blanks are retained. This makes it ideal for text that is formatted with columns such as numeric tables or any text where spacing must be preserved. Horizontal tabs are recognized and expanded as if there are tab stops every eight characters across the page.

Like other block elements, preformatted text implies a paragraph break before and after the defining tags. Within the preformatted block no other structure tags should be used. Style tags are appropriate, as are anchor and image tags. Here's a simple example of preformatted text:

```
<HEAD>
<TITLE>Preformatted Text example</TITLE>
```

```
</HEAD>

<BODY>
<H2>Puzzle</H2>
<PRE>
                              |\   /
        Here's one way to     o o o
           connect all 9      |  X
        dots using only 4     o o o
           straight lines:    |/   \
                              o-o-o-
</PRE>

</BODY>
```

This will create the display shown in Figure 2.7.

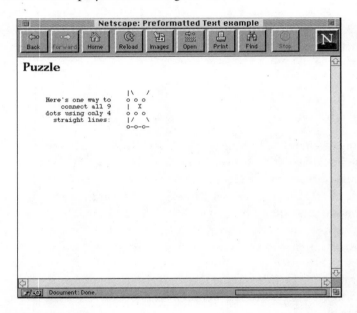

Figure 2.7: Preformatted text

The preformatted tag has one optional attribute, WIDTH. When specified, the WIDTH attribute tells the browser the maximum line length that can be expected within the preformatted text. With this information the browser can adjust the margins or font size to accommodate the text. Values of either 40, 80, or 132 should be used for best results. Example:

```
<PRE WIDTH=80> this is preformatted text</PRE>
```

LISTS

A list is a structured paragraph containing a sequence of list items. HTML provides three kinds of lists: ordered, unordered, and definition lists. Ordered lists have numbered items, unordered lists have bulleted items. Each item on either of these two lists is enclosed in list item tags, <LI></LI>. Ordered lists use the <OL></OL> tags to enclose and mark the entire list structure, unordered lists use <UL></UL> tags. When rendered by the browser, list items are usually indented a short bit in from the left margin.

Definition lists have, as each item of the list, a pair of objects called the definition term and definition description. The definition term is enclosed in the <DT></DT> tags and is rendered aligned to the left margin. The definition description is enclosed in the <DD></DD> tags and is rendered indented from the left margin. The entire definition list is enclosed with the tags <DL> and </DL>. No number or bullets are added. Definition lists are very powerful. I'll have more about them further on.

Lists can be nested, making them ideal for implementing outlines and tables of contents. Other than nesting, however, you should not use any other tags in an ordered or unordered list item that imply paragraph breaks, such as headings, horizontal rules, tables, or forms; images and links are just fine. Here's an example using ordered and unordered lists:

```
<HEAD>
<TITLE>Examples of Lists</TITLE>
</HEAD>
<BODY>
<H1 ALIGN=center>HTML Book</H1>
<HR>
<!-- USE HEADINGS FOR MAJOR SECTIONS -->
<H2>Table of Contents</H2>
<H3>Chapters</H3>
<OL>
    <LI>Introduction</LI>
    <LI>The Language</LI>
    <!—USE BULLETS FOR THIS LEVEL—>
    <UL>
        <LI>Syntax</LI>
```

```
        <LI>Formatting</LI>
     </UL>
     <LI>Writing Documents</LI>
  </OL>
  <HR>
  </BODY>
```

Figure 2.8 shows how this example looks.

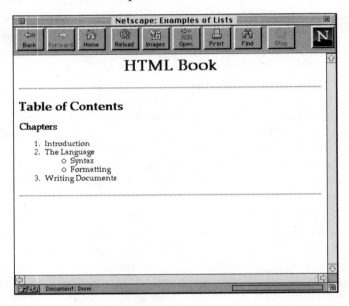

Figure 2.8: Ordered and unordered listst

The indentations used above are only there to make the HTML easier to read; in no way do they affect how a browser formats the text. Note that the nested unordered list appears between two ordered list items; not inside an item. In other words, it would be incorrect to write:

```
<LI>
<UL>
<LI>Syntax</LI>
<LI>Formatting</LI>
</UL>
</LI>
```

In HTML2, the list item tag was empty, so you are likely to find many pages on the World Wide Web where list items are missing the closing </LI> tag in the HTML source. They still work. Also, in the HTML 2.0 specification, there were two additional kinds of lists which used the list item tag: the menu list, using the <MENU></MENU> tags, and the directory list with <DIR></DIR> tags. The menu list was intended for lists of short items, rendered more compactly than <UL> and the directory list for lists of very short elements, such as file names, rendered in multiple columns. Both these lists are functionally replaced in HTML3 by new attributes to the ordered and unordered lists tags. Therefore, while still supported, <MENU></MENU> and <DIR></DIR> are no longer recommended to authors.

Both ordered and unordered lists can have the COMPACT attribute which should render a list with less line spacing between items. Also, both lists can have the PLAIN attribute to specify that no bullets or numbers be affixed to the list items. <OL PLAIN COMPACT> is the substitute tag for <MENU>, and to get multiple columns for directory lists, <UL PLAIN WRAP=horiz> is used.

In HTML2, it was common to use a heading as a title or caption for a list. HTML3 added the list header tags, <LH></LH>, to enclose text for use as a list heading.

Ordered lists have two attributes for control over the sequencing of list items. SEQNUM can be used to set the number for the first item to some value other than one. CONTINUE instructs the browser not to restart numbering but to continue where the previous list left off.

Netscape previously added similiar attributes to the ordered and unordered list elements, TYPE and START. For ordered lists, TYPE can take the following values:

TYPE="1"	Normal numeric numbering; the default
TYPE="A"	Uppercase letters; A, B, C, D, ...
TYPE="a"	Lowercase letters; a, b, c, d, ...
TYPE="I"	Uppercase Roman numerals; I, II, III, IV, ...
TYPE="i"	Lowercase Roman numerals; i, ii, iii, iv, ...

The value of the START attribute is a number indicating with which value list numbering should start. It is equivalent to the HTML3 SEQNUM attribute.

For unordered lists, the TYPE attribute can take the values "circle", "square", or "disc" to indicate the type of bullet used. The START attribute is ignored in unordered lists.

In contrast to ordered and unordered lists, a definition list has no restrictions regarding the use of other HTML elements within either the defining term or description part. This is what makes it such a powerful element. Let's start with a simple example of a definition list.

```
<H2>Cast of Characters</H2>
<DL>
<DT>Orsino</DT><DD>Duke of Illyria.</DD>
<DT>Sebastian</DT><DD>Brother to Viola.</DD>
<DT>Antonio</DT><DD>A sea captain, friend to Sebastian.</DD>
<DT>Fabian</DT><DD>A pop star of the early 'sixties.</DD>
</DL>
```

Figure 2.9 shows how this example looks on the screen.

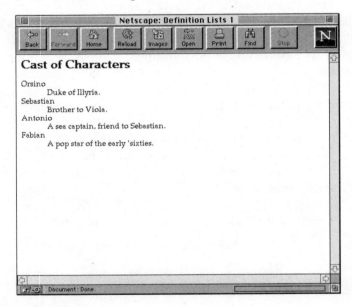

Figure 2.9: Simple definition list

Note that there's no white space inserted between the term and description. A common technique is to make the term a heading, that is,

```
<DL>
<DT><H3>Bucky Balls</H3></DT>
<DD>Technically, Buckminster Fullerene, a family of all carbon
molecules named after the great designer-architect-engineer,
Buckminster Fuller. The most stable member, C60, is a
hollow sphere with the same architecture as the geodesic structures
```

```
Fuller pioneered a half century ago.</DD>
<DT><H3>Penrose Tiling</H3></DT>
<DD>A method of tiling a plane thought impossible until discovered by
Dr. Roger Penrose. Combining two differently shaped rhomboids,
the tiling has five-fold symmetry, yet <EM>the pattern is not
periodic!</EM>. A mathematical curiosity until it was found in
some natural minerals with rather strange properties.</DD>
</DL>
```

As can be seen in Figure 2.10, this technique visually emphasizes each list item.

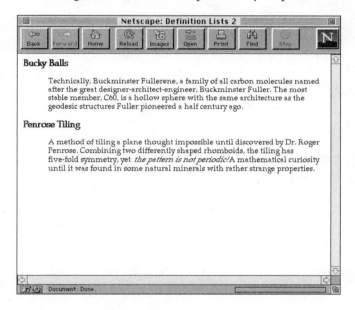

Figure 2.10: Definition list with headings

TABLES

Often there's a need to present information in a more structured fashion than that provided by lists. Tables allow you to display information organized into rows and columns. Tables are a HTML3 feature that was implemented early by Netscape Navigator. Previous to their introduction, it was necessary to use the preformatted text element using tabs to align columns of data. This is still an acceptable way to present simple tables, especially tables of numeric data where the fixed width font imposed by the <PRE></PRE> tags doesn't look so bad.

Spreadsheet data, exported in tab-delimited format, can be directly included in a Web page in this manner.

There are horizontal tabs in HTML3. The empty tag, <TAB>, is used to both define tab stops and to move the print position. Horizontal tabs provide an easy way to line up simple data in columns.

To create a tab stop at the current position in the text, use the ID attribute, for example: <TAB ID="t1">. Then to move the print position, use the TO attribute: <TAB TO="t1">. The ALIGN attribute controls the behavior of the tab stop and the INDENT ATTRIBUTE lets you move the print position a specific number of en units. The en is a typographical unit equal to half the point size of the current font. The following bit of HTML illustrates using tabs to align data in columns.

```
<H4>The Inner Planets</H4>
<P><B>
<TAB INDENT=20 ID="t1" ALIGN=char>Distance (Aus)
<TAB INDENT=20 ID="t2" ALIGN=right>Length - Year
<TAB INDENT=20 ID="t3" ALIGN=right>Length - Day
</B><BR>
<B>Mercury</B>
<TAB TO="t1"> 0.38<TAB TO="t2"> 88 dys<TAB TO="t3"> 59 dys<BR>
<B>Venus</B>
<TAB TO="t1"> 0.72<TAB TO="t2"> 225 dys<TAB TO="t3"> 243 dys<BR>
<B>Earth</B>
<TAB TO="t1"> 1.00<TAB TO="t2"> 365 dys<TAB TO="t3"> 24 hrs<BR>
<B>Mars</B>
<TAB TO="t1"> 1.52<TAB TO="t2"> 687 dys<TAB TO="t3"> 25 hrs
</P>
```

Figure 2.11 shows how this would look in a browser. Note how the first Tab stop is specified with ALIGN=char. This will align text on the decimal point character of the currently defined language. The CHAR attribute can be used to specify a different alignment character, for example:

```
<TAB ID="email" ALIGN=char CHAR="@">
```

For more complex requirements, the table element is preferred. Tables are defined as a series of rows each containing a series of cells. This model allows cells to span multiple rows or columns. The rows can be grouped into a table head and one or more table body sections. For large tables, browsers can keep the table head static while table body parts scroll underneath.

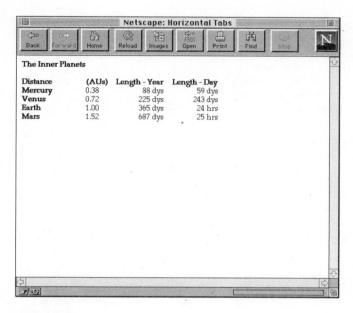

Figure 2.11: Horizontal tabs

Table cells come in two varieties: header cells and data cells. By default, data cell content is rendered in normal left-justified text, while header cell content is rendered in boldfaced text and centered. A table cell can contain any other HTML elements—lists, images, headings—even other tables.

A table begins and ends with the <TABLE></TABLE> tags. Table rows are defined by <TR></TR>; header cells by <TH></TH>; and data cells by <TD></TD>. A table must have at least one row and one cell. An optional table sub-element, <CAPTION></CAPTION> supplies—you guessed it— a caption for the table. The caption is in bold type and, by default, centered above the table. Figure 2.12 shows the simple 3-row by 3-column table generated by the following HTML:

```
<TABLE>
<CAPTION>Total Table Items</CAPTION>
<TR><TH></TH> <TH>Lunch</TH> <TH>Dinner</TH></TR>
<TR><TH>Kitchen</TH> <TD>23</TD> <TD>30</TD></TR>
<TR><TH>Dining Room</TH> <TD>31</TD> <TD>45</TD></TR>
</TABLE>
```

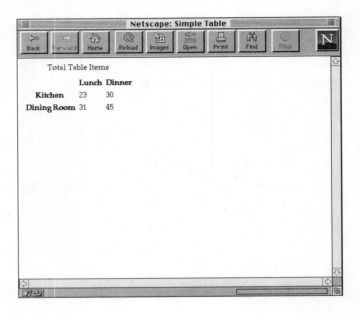

Figure 2.12: Basic table

Netscape Navigator implemented tables about half a year before the HTML3 specification for tables was set. Fortunately, many of the table attributes implemented by Netscape have been adopted into the HTML3 specification. The complete set of table attributes and sub-elements is robust. Many different styles of tables can be achieved. Let's start with Netscape's extensions, as they provide one method of control of the table layout and progress from there to the more powerful methods provided by HTML3.

The ALIGN attribute is supported in the table tag and the sub-elements <THEAD>, <TBODY>, <TR>, <TH>, and <TD> with the standard values of left, center, and right. Tables normally occupy the full width of the browser's display window. The ALIGN attribute should be used in the <TABLE> tag in conjunction with the WIDTH attribute to control the placement of the table with respect to the display, for example, <TABLE ALIGN=center WIDTH=50%>. When specified in the <CAPTION> tag, ALIGN is either top (the default) or bottom, and controls where the caption appears: either above or below the table.

ALIGN, specified with the other table elements, controls the placement of the contents within table cells. The allowed values are: left, center, right, justify, and char. Alignment specified at the table cell level has precedence over row alignment, which has precedence over table body or head alignment. Conversely, alignment is inherited from the head/body level if not specified at the row level and cell alignment is inherited from the row level if not specified at the cell level.

The VALIGN attribute is similiar. It can have the values top, middle, or bottom, and controls the vertical positioning of table cell contents. The default is middle. Obviously, the more complex the content of a data cell the more careful you should be using ALIGN and VALIGN.

The <TABLE> tag can have these additional attributes; the value, represented by "n" in each case, is a whole number of screen pixels:

- ▸ BORDER=n   The table is displayed in a rectangle with n-pixel weight lines defining table cell walls. The default is BORDER=0.

- ▸ CELLPADDING=n   The table will be rendered with n pixels space between the contents of the table's cells and the walls of the cells.

- ▸ CELLSPACING=n   The table will be rendered with cell walls n pixels thick.

At the data cell level, Netscape's table implementation provided the attributes, ROWSPAN and COLSPAN for a little more control. Here's an example showing how these can be used:

```
<TABLE CELLPADDING=5 BORDER=2>
<CAPTION ALIGN=bottom>The Inner Planets</CAPTION>
<TR><TH ROWSPAN=2></TH>
 <TH COLSPAN=2>Distance from Sun</TH>
 <TH ROWSPAN=2>Year<BR>Length</TH>
 <TH ROWSPAN=2>Day<BR>length</TH> </TR>
<TR><!-- spanned cell -->
 <TH>kilometers</TH><TH>AUs</TH>
 <!-- 2 spanned cells --> </TR>
<TR><TH>Mercury</TH>
 <TD>57,900,000</TD> <TD>.38</TD> <TD>88 days</TD> <TD>59 days</TD></TR>
<TR><TH>Venus</TH>
 <TD>108,200,000</TD> <TD>.72</TD> <TD>225 days</TD> <TD>243
days</TD></TR>
<TR><TH>Earth</TH>
 <TD>149,600,000</TD> <TD>1.0</TD> <TD>365 days</TD> <TD>24
hrs</TD></TR>
<TR><TH>Mars</TH>
```

```
<TD>227,900,000</TD> <TD>1.5</TD> <TD>687 days</TD> <TD>24.6
hrs</TD></TR>
</TABLE>
```

The HTML3 table model permits additional attributes to be specified with the <TABLE> tag:

- ▶ FLOAT   With a value of either right or left, specifies text flow with the table positioned to the right or left of the text following the closing </TABLE> tag. The default is no text flow.

- ▶ COLS=n   Specifies the number of table columns. By knowing this number in advance, a browser can determine the table layout faster.

- ▶ FRAME   Values are: none, top, bottom, topbot, sides, and all, giving control over individual elements of the table's outer border.

- ▶ RULES   Values are: none, basic, rows, cols, and all, for control over individual elements of the cell grid.

The defaults for FRAME and RULES are none if the BORDER attribute is absent or has a zero value, and all If BORDER has a positive value.

Within the table element, HTML3 has new sub-elements. The <THEAD></THEAD> and <TBODY></TBODY> tags permit the application of alignment and class attribute values to subsections of the table. The empty <COL> tag provides a convenient means of applying attributes to one or more columns of the table. There should be one <COL> tag for each table column. Alternatively, SPAN can be used to have the other attributes apply to a series of columns. For example, the table shown in Figure 2.13 could be more precisely specified by adding

```
<COL><COL ALIGN=right><COL ALIGN=char><COL SPAN=2 ALIGN=char CHAR=" ">
```

right after the caption tags. For even more control, the CLASS attribute can be added and associated with a class name in a style sheet to have columns rendered in different font families or even different colors.

STYLES

Style tags change the typography of contained text. Style tags can be nested within other style tags in the same manner as you would apply type styles in a word processing program. However, HTML styles are abstract or logical constructs, whereas the styles used in word processing programs are explicit. Most other markup tags can occur within style tags, though the use of structural

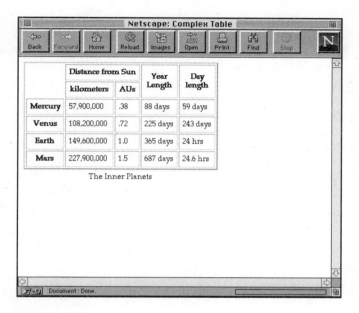

Figure 2.13: Complex table

elements inside of a style should generally be avoided. Here are the most common style tags from HTML2:

- ▶ `<EM></EM>` Emphasis, usually rendered in italic or underlined to bring out the text slightly from the background text

- ▶ `<STRONG></STRONG>` Strong emphasis, usually rendered in boldface. Must be rendered differently from emphasis

- ▶ `<CITE></CITE>` Citation, for titles and references within the text, typically rendered in italic

- ▶ `</TT>` Typewriter Text, a monospaced font (every character has the same width) such as Courier is used

Figure 2.14 shows the result of using the above text in a definition list.

HTML does include explicit styles, specifically the tags, `<B></B>`, `<I></I>`, and `<U></U>`, for, respectively, bold, italic, and underlined text, for those instances where exact control is required—for example, when one part of the text must refer to other parts (such as "Optional rules are specified in italics"). Authors are encouraged, however, to use the logical style tags wherever possible to provide greater consistency among documents from different sources.

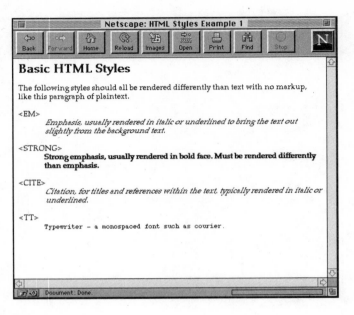

Figure 2.14: Styles

Following are most of the other style tags recognized by the majority of browsers. Different browsers will render these styles differently, and many browsers will not render each style in a way distinct from all other styles.

- ▶ <ABBREV></ABBREV>   Identifies an abbreviation
- ▶ <ACRONYM></ACRONYM>   Identifies an acronym
- ▶ <AU></AU>   The author or, perhaps, just an author
- ▶ <BIG></BIG>   Designates that a font somewhat larger than the current size should be used
- ▶ <DEL></DEL>   Marks deleted content that remains, ghostlike, for reference purposes
- ▶ <DFN></DFN>   Defining instance, used to mark the introduction of a new term
- ▶ <INS></INS>   Denotes new text, inserted in the content
- ▶ <PERSON></PERSON>   Marks, for emphasis, the name of a person

- ► </Q> Encloses the contained text in quotation marks appropriate to the current language
- ► </S> Strikethrough text, as in legal documents. This replaces <STRIKE></STRIKE> in HTML2
- ► <SMALL></SMALL> Indicates that a font somewhat smaller in size than the current size should be used
- ► Subscript. The text is lowered and may be rendered with a smaller font size than normal.
- ► Superscript. The text is raised and may be rendered with a smaller font size than normal.

For manuals, computer system documentation, and user's guides:

- ► <CODE></CODE> Coding—For samples of computer programming, usually rendered in a monospaced font.
- ► <VAR></VAR> Variable—In instructional text, the name of a value to be supplied by the user
- ► <KBD></KBD> Keyboard—A sequence of characters to be typed in, exactly, by the user
- ► <SAMP></SAMP> Sample—A sequence of literal characters

Netscape navigator recognizes a special style tag, FONT, which is written with the SIZE attribute. The SIZE attribute can have a positive or negative value from 1 to 7 specifying that the enclosed text be rendered in a font size larger or smaller than the size currently in effect. This is an easy way to fake a small caps font. For example:

```
<FONT SIZE=+3>K</FONT>OOL TRIC<FONT SIZE=+3>K</FONT>
```

And, finally, there's one other Netscape only tag that should be used sparingly, if at all: the <BLINK></BLINK> element.

ANCHORS AND LINKS

Anchors are the parts of the page—those blue underlined bits—that, when clicked on, take the reader somewhere else. Anchors are what link Web pages together. The anchor tag has one prime attribute, HREF—Hypertext REFerence. The element is usually written:

```
<A HREF="some_url">Go to some URL</A>
```

The value of the HREF attribute is a Uniform Resource Locator, or URL. In the simplest format, where both the start and the destination of the link are within the same document, the value of the HREF attribute is a name preceded by a pound sign. For example:

```
Addresses of <A HREF="#sources">additional sources</A>
can be found at the end of this chapter.
  *

  *

<P ID="sources">Finally, some more sources of information.</P>
```

Older browsers may not recognize the ID attribute in all contexts. These browsers expect a name to be defined by an anchor tag with the NAME attribute; that is,

```
<P><A NAME="sources">Finally, some more sources of information.</A></P>
```

Clicking on the phrase "additional sources" will command the browser to jump to the named section somewhere else in the document.

The URL format permits almost any resource on the Internet to be addressed, whether that resource is an HTML file on a Web server or some other Internet resource, such as a gopher server or a Usenet newsgroup. The URL has several parts, not all of which are required in order for the URL to be valid. In order of appearance, they specify the

- ▶ Method to be used to access the resource
- ▶ Name of the server providing the resource
- ▶ Port number to be used on the server
- ▶ Directory path to the resource
- ▶ File name of the resource
- ▶ Named element in the HTML document

The parts above are separated by various delimiters and the whole is enclosed in quotes, as follows:

```
"method://server:port/path/file#anchor"
```

The port number is sort of like the telephone extension number of the server. Most URLs you find do not include a port number since most servers use the defaults.

To link to another HTML document in the same directory as the current one, only the file name is needed; all the missing information is taken from the current document. This is called relative URL addressing and it should be used for creating any links to documents within the Webspace. The following example provides a link to a file spot_info.html:

```
His cat is named <A HREF="spot_info.html">Spot</A>.
```

Relative addressing gives your hypertext work portability since as long as the files stay together in the same logical directory, none of the relative links need to be respecified when the collection is moved from one server to another. To link to a specific anchor in the destination page, follow the file name with a pound sign and the name of the anchor, like this:

```
<A HREF="spot_info.html#habits">Spot</A>
```

Suppose the file is in a subdirectory of the directory of the current file; say, one named pets. A link to the file above would be written:

```
<A HREF="pets/spot_info.html">Spot</A>
```

It makes no difference how directory paths and file names are actually constructed in the operating system under which the server is running—whether backslashes separate directories, as in Windows, or square brackets are used, as in VMS—URL syntax uses slashes for all these forms. The server will be responsible for converting the request to the actual form used to reference the file.

If the file is on a different server than that of the current file, then the access method and the domain name of the server must be specified, separated by double slashes. Here's an example:

```
<A
HREF="http://www.enterprise.ufp.mil/officers/data/spot_info.html
">Spot</A>
```

This is called full URL addressing. The only assumption made is that the Web server, www.enterprise.ufp.mil, is running on port 80, which is the default port for World Wide Web servers. If this is not the case—say, www.enterprise.ufp.mil is on port 1080—then the port must be specified as follows:

```
<A
HREF="http://enterprise.ufp.mil:1080/officers/data/spot_info.htm
l">Spot</A>
```

As you can see, URLs can be quite lengthy.

Other resources on the Internet besides HTML documents can be linked from an HTML document. The general philosophy is if it's out there, you can construct an URL to point to it. Specific methods exist for ftp, gopher, news, and WAIS servers, and for accessing Telnet sessions. Browsers will take different actions depending on the type of resource accessed.

Here are some examples of Internet URLs:

```
ftp://ftp.uu.net/doc/literary/obi/World.Factbook
gopher://gopher.micro.umn.edu/
telnet://compuserve.com/
news:alt.cows.moo
```

A gopher is assumed to be on the default gopher port, port 70. If the gopher uses another port, it must be specified by following the server name with a colon and the number. If an URL for a gopher or ftp resource ends in a specific file name, then that file is downloaded to the reader's computer. If the URL points to a directory, then the directory will be displayed by the browser in a standard format with links for subdirectories and files. You can add a TITLE attribute to an anchor tag to provide a title for this display window.

The format for accessing Usenet newsgroups, as you can see, is different from the format for accessing other Internet resources in that it does not specify a news (NNTP) server. The server name is set somewhere else, typically somewhere in the browser's preferences dialog. The idea is that, theoretically, all NNTP servers have the same content, so the server choice should be left up to the reader.

INLINE IMAGES

An image or two will go a long way in making your Web page more attractive. The images on your home page will give information to the reader that cannot be gleaned from the text; a simple line graph is more informative than a table of numbers. Images function importantly as page design elements.

To include an inline image in your page, use the empty image tag, <IMG>. No paragraph breaks or other white space around the image are implied. If text flow around the image is not specified, then the image is inserted into the text like a single odd-sized character. Unlike an image in a page layout program, which can be anchored to a specific spot on the page, an inline image on a Web page is part of the text in which it is embedded. Anywhere that you can place a character of text, you can put an inline image.

The image tag has three important attributes:

- ▸ SRC—The source attribute is mandatory. Its value is the URL of the file containing the image to be embedded. Specify the URL in the same way as that of the HREF attribute used in the anchor tag.

- ▸ ALIGN—For an inline image, one of three values: top, middle, or bottom, to define how the image should be aligned with the adjacent text and other HTML elements.

- ▸ ALT—The ALT attribute is used to specify a text string that can be displayed if the image is not available or the reader has chosen not to load images.

Netscape introduced additional image tag attributes to permit content to flow around the left or right side of an image. HTML3 has a different approach using the figure element. These features and imagemaps are discussed in Chapter 5.

Here's an example of a page with two small, inline images; the second image is the anchor of a link:

```
<HEAD>
<TITLE>Image Example</TITLE>
</HEAD>
<BODY>
<H1>Inline Images</H1>
<P><IMG SRC="Mosaic.GIF"> Mosaic was the first graphical browser
capable of displaying in-line images.</P>
<P>Need <A HREF="http://www.ncsa.uiuc.edu/Mosaic/QuickStart.html">
<IMG SRC="More.GIF" ALT=" more " ALIGN=middle> information</A>?</P>
</BODY>
```

Figure 2.15 shows how this would be displayed.

In the above example, both images are decorative—the page would function just as well without them. A browser that could not display the image would substitute the word "more," specified as the value of the ALT attribute, as the anchor of the line. Note that the example has spaces before and after the image tag. They are used here because the browser regards inline images as odd-sized characters in the text, and, in word-wrapping the paragraphs, we want the inline images to behave as one-letter words rather than be attached to adjacent text.

There is, of course, a lot more to putting images on a Web page. In Chapter 5 you'll find a discussion of text flow around images and figures, imagemaps with clickable areas, and some of the tricks you can do with image loading and placement.

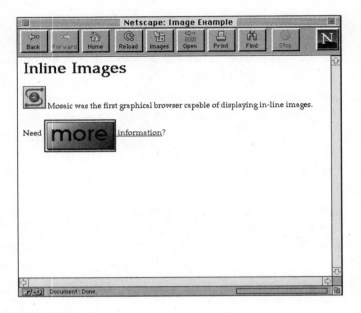

Figure 2.15: Inline images

FORMS

Interactive forms allow you to obtain information from your readers. An interactive form on a Web page is very much like a reader reply card bound into a magazine. The reader types information into fields on the form. When done, the contents of the form are posted somewhere for processing; either to an e-mail address or to a script on a server. Sending the contents to a server has advantages—the information can be checked and processed in real time and a custom reply can be generated (possibly containing another form) and returned to the reader. Having the form contents sent to an e-mail address has the advantage that you don't need to run a server in order to test the form and you don't have to write a program to process the input. Such programs, known as common gateway interface (cgi) scripts, are written in various languages—UNIX Shell, PERL, TCL, C, AppleScript—for different operating systems and writing them requires a level of programming expertise that's beyond the skills necessary to author Web pages. Cgi scripts are discussed in more detail in Chapter 6. The examples in this section post the contents to an e-mail address.

A form is a designated area of an HTML page, often rendered with a surrounding border, containing input fields and other interactive objects, such as pop-up menus, checkboxes, and buttons. There can be any number of forms on a page each beginning and ending with the tags, <FORM> and </FORM>. The beginning FORM tag takes an ACTION attribute that specifies what should be done with the information entered by the reader. The ACTION attribute takes an URL as its value which can either be the URL of a cgi script or a "mailto" URL, as in the example:

```
<FORM METHOD=post ACTION="mailto:president@whitehouse.gov">
```

Be aware that some older browsers may not support mailto URLs and that a browser must be properly configured for it to work properly. The following example, shown in Figure 2.16, illustrates a simple form application to request a comment from the reader:

```
<HEAD>
<TITLE>Form Example</TITLE>
</HEAD>
<BODY>
<H1>Comments Please</H1>
<P>We would like to hear from you. Please use the following form to
submit any comments on our service.</P>
<FORM METHOD="post" ACTION="mailto:mybox@myplace.com">
<P>Please enter your name: <INPUT TYPE="text" NAME="name" SIZE="30"><BR>
and your email address: <INPUT TYPE="text" NAME="addr" SIZE="30"></P>
<HR>
<P>Use the input area below to enter any comments you like.<BR>
Click the SUBMIT button when you are done.</P>
<TEXTAREA NAME="comment" ROWS=6 COLS=40></TEXTAREA>
<P>Thanks for your input.
<INPUT TYPE="submit"> <INPUT TYPE="reset"></P>
</FORM>
</BODY>
```

First, note that other HTML elements can be freely used inside and outside the form. The opening FORM tag has two attributes. The first, METHOD, indicates how the form's content will be presented to the script or e-mailer. Always use the value "post" to specify that the content is presented as standard input. The other value, GET, is obsolete. It specifies that the form's content is sent to the server in the form of an URL. Some older servers limit the length of data passed this way, so use post. The ACTION attribute says to post the contents of the form to the e-mail address: mybox@myplace.com.

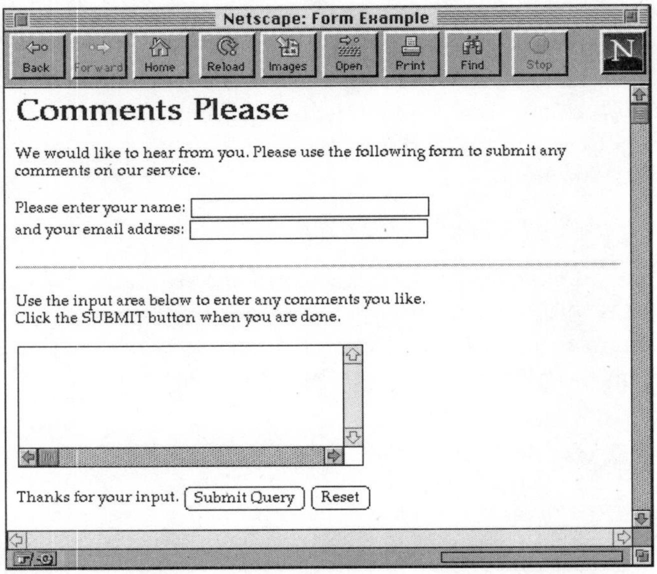

Figure 2.16: Simple input form

The first two fields in the example request the reader's name and e-mail address with INPUT tags. INPUT tags are empty; like IMAGE tags, INPUT tags insert objects inline with other text that word-wraps normally with that text. The TYPE attribute of the input tags in this example has the value, "text", indicating a single line field whose length in characters is given by the SIZE attribute. Each input tag must have a NAME attribute with a unique value within the form.

The TEXTAREA tag signals the placement of an input area with a specified number of rows and columns, allowing the reader to enter free-form text. Unlike the INPUT tag, the TEXTAREA tag is not empty; any text between it and the ending tag, "</TEXTAREA>", is used to initialize the text area for reader editing. In this example, the text area is left blank.

At the end of the form are two buttons created by the tags <INPUT TYPE="submit"> and <INPUT TYPE="reset">. When clicked, the submit button signals the browser to take the action specified in the FORM tag—sending the contents of the fields to the specified e-mail address. The reset button will, when clicked, clear all input fields within the enclosing FORM tags.

What gets mailed to the address? It's a string with each input field presented as name=value separated with an ampersand. The name is from the INPUT tag's NAME attribute and the value is from the reader's input. If I had typed in my name and e-mail address in the example shown in Figure 2.16, and in the TEXTAREA field typed, "Just checking!", the body of an e-mail message sent to mybox@myplace.com would contain:

```
name=Larry+Aronson&addr=laronson@acm.org&comment=Just+checking%21
```

Trailing blanks are trimmed from the input field and the plus sign is substituted for any internal blank. Special characters, such as the exclamation point at the end of the comment, are represented by hexadecimal values escaped with the percent sign (%21 = decimal 33 = ASCII "!"). Most computer languages have a built-in command or function to convert hex values to characters.

When you want the reader to enter a value from a finite list of options, there are radio buttons, checkboxes, and pop-up menus at your disposal.

Radio buttons operate in a set such that when one is selected, all other buttons in the set are deselected. Radio buttons should be used when the choice is one-and-only-one from a small set of mutually exclusive values. Each button is defined with a separate input tag, however, the NAME attribute has the same value for all buttons in the set. For example:

```
<H3>Annual Income Level:</H3>
<P>
<INPUT TYPE="radio" NAME="income" VALUE=1> $0 to $19,999<BR>
<INPUT TYPE="radio" NAME="income" VALUE=2 CHECKED> $20,000 to
$59,999<BR>
<INPUT TYPE="radio" NAME="income" VALUE=3> $60,000 and up
</P>
```

Checkboxes are used when the choice is zero-or-many from a small set of nonexclusive values. Each box is defined with a separate input tag and, since checkboxes are not grouped into sets, each has a unique value for the NAME attribute. For example:

```
<H3>Computers:</H3>
<P>
<INPUT TYPE="checkbox" NAME="C1" VALUE="W"> Windows
<INPUT TYPE="checkbox" NAME="C2" VALUE="M"> Macintosh
<INPUT TYPE="checkbox" NAME="C3" VALUE="U"> UNIX
<INPUT TYPE="checkbox" NAME="C4" VALUE="O"> Other
</P>
```

Pop-up menus are created with the SELECT tag. Pop-up menus are useful for having the reader choose one option from a set of many; it is a container and the individual options are marked with <OPTION></OPTION> tags as in this example:

```
<H3>Primary Application:</H3>

<P>
<SELECT NAME="prime">
<OPTION SELECTED>Word Processing</OPTION>
<OPTION>Graphics</OPTION>
<OPTION>Spread Sheet</OPTION>
<OPTION>Project Management</OPTION>
<OPTION>Games</OPTION>
<OPTION>Utilities</OPTION>
<OPTION>Programming</OPTION>
<OPTION>Database</OPTION>
</SELECT>
</P>
```

One of the options in a SELECT should have the SELECTED attribute, otherwise, by default, the first OPTION value is selected. Multiple choices can be specified by adding the attribute MULTIPLE to the SELECT tag. The content of each OPTION is the value that will be posted should the reader choose that option, for example, prime=Games. This can be overridden by adding VALUE attributes to the OPTION tags, for example,

```
<OPTION VALUE="pman">Project Management</OPTION>
```

Figure 2.17 shows radio buttons, checkboxes and pop-up menus in use.

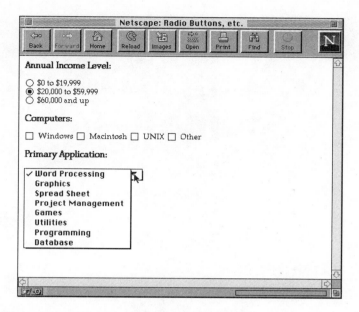

Figure 2.17: Radio buttons, checkboxes, and pop-up menus

Writing HTML Documents

General HTML principles

Approaches to writing Web pages

Good HTML Style

Common mistakes

I f you've gone through the previous chapter you should now know enough to start gathering your content (text and images) together and marking it up into Web pages. Webspace development is always done locally. You can create HTML files with a wide variety of software, from simple text editors to sophisticated HTML authoring environments. The files are opened and checked with your favorite browser. It's an iterative process—rechecking and making corrections until you get it right, then uploading directories and files from your desktop or portable PC to a Web server.

You can put information on the World Wide Web very quickly. In a day or two, you can get up the core of a Website that will establish a solid presence for you or your organization on the Web. However, it's just as easy to create a sloppy hypertext work as it is to create a neat one. In this chapter you'll find a discussion of the principles of writing good Web pages and some common mistakes to avoid.

The art and practice of Web publishing is rapidly growing and changing. New technologies and techniques are introduced and spread rapidly. Although you can write a simple home page in a few hours, you'll never be finished with it—Web pages are living documents that grow and change as you do. This is one reason observing a few principles of good design can be so important. The creation of a personal home page, in particular, is an act of creative expression in a brand new medium. It is the setting up of your booth in cyberspace to provide information, goods, and services, and to define who you are to the Global Electronic Village.

General HTML principles

Another reason good design is so important with Web applications is that you have no control over the context from which people will establish links to pages in your Webspace. Think of your Webspace as a house in cyberspace; the door is always open. Each HTML page is a room in this house. Most people will enter via your home page—the front door. A good home page serves to properly welcome its visitors and let them know where they are and what interesting resources are to be found inside. The browsers' navigation controls will let readers exit the way they came in; still, it's nice when the home page provides suggestions and links to other places in cyberspace to visit.

Not everybody will enter your Webspace through its home page. Some people will come in through the windows of other rooms in your cyberspace house. There are a number of automated programs that continually explore the Web. These programs, variously called robots, spiders, worms, or Webwalkers, link from one Web server to another—building databases of titles, headings, and URLs as they go. There are many Web sites from which you can search these databases (check the "Internet Search" item under Netscape Navigator's Directory menu). For example, you could search for all Web pages that have the word "fractal" in their titles and the result would be a dynamically generated page of links. Such links are independent of the structure intended by the authors of those pages. The point is that readers will find ways you didn't anticipate to enter your hypertext work. Help these people out: As a minimum, provide a link back to your home page from every other page you put on the Web. Don't leave lost readers feeling more lost than when they entered.

Hypertext works on the Web are living, growing structures. The best Webspaces provide the reader with the feeling of visiting a real place occupied and maintained by an interesting community of people. Keep this in mind, and with a little preparation, practice, and planning, your pages can grow and evolve as part of the World Wide Web.

The best preparation for writing HTML documents for the Web is reading Web HTML documents. Get a feel for what other authors have put on the Web and the approaches they've taken in organizing and formatting their work. At this writing, somewhere around two-thirds of all people surfing the Web are using Netscape Navigator, and many Web pages are designed specifically for that browser and the expanded set of HTML elements it accepts. If you don't have Netscape Navigator, I highly recommend that you get it. Information on obtaining Netscape Navigator is available at <http://www.netscape.com/>. Get some other browsers as well. NCSA Mosaic and CERN's Arena browser are also important standards. Internet Explorer, Microsoft Network's brother, as well as America Online and CompuServe's browsers are handy for checking your Web pages.

Most browsers come set to load a default home page—usually a home page of the manufacturing company or organization. This is a good place to start your study of Web pages. Another good place is NCSA's What's New page at <http://www.ncsa.uiuc.edu/SDG/Software/Mosaic/Docs/whats-new.html>. This page is updated every two weeks with links to Web pages that have just been created. It's a good sampling of what people in many different fields are doing right now on the Web. If you want to explore the Web focusing on a specific subject, Yahoo is an excellent subject-oriented catalog. I recommend creating a bookmark or hotlist item for Yahoo. The URL is <http://www.yahoo.com/>.

Most graphical Web browsers allow you to view and save any page on the Web in its original form (in computer terms—the source code) as an HTML file. It is then a simple matter to open that file in a text editor to see how the author used HTML to create the page seen in the browser's window. (Depending on your browser, you may have to set an option or preference to use your favorite text editor instead of the default viewer provided.) As practice in writing HTML documents, edit these files and change the tags. Select the Open Local… choice under your browser's File menu to view the re-edited pages and see your changes. After looking at a number of HTML documents and playing with the different elements of HTML, you should start to have an idea of what you can do with your own applications. But before you start, it's good to review a few principles that apply to computer projects in general but have special application to writing HTML documents for the World Wide Web.

GENERAL PRINCIPLE NUMBER ONE

Keep it simple. Emphasize content over form. You have little control over the typography and layout your document will have when viewed by the various browsers readers have at their disposal, so don't waste a lot of effort trying to get something to look just right. Keep your pages as simple as possible and they will look good everywhere. Spend your time making the content—the information you want to convey to the reader—clear and compelling. Your pages will grow and change over time. It's better to start simply and have the evolving content drive the design of the page than to have an overdesigned page constrain the evolving content. If the typography of a document must be exact, consider providing alternative versions on your Web server in formats that readers can download and display offline—a Microsoft Word document in RTF (rich text format) or an Adobe PostScript or Acrobat file, for example.

Make sure the images on your Web page are informative. A small picture of you on your home page provides readers with information that words alone cannot convey. A picture of your computer, unless you've done something extraordinary by transforming it into a work of art, does not. Avoid putting up Web pages that emulate automated teller machines with large graphical buttons for links. They take too long to load and are harder to maintain. An HTML list or table element should do to organize any set of links and their use creates a more consistent style between Webspaces. Small icons can be used to decorate the page, adding personality and visual clues for navigation.

A Web page should not look like a magazine cover, either. Web pages are not in competition with each other for the reader's attention as in other media. Readers will choose to link to your page because they are browsing related information. A Web page does not have to depend as much on eye-grabbing graphics and promotion to reach readers as do magazines sitting on a shelf. I don't mean to imply that you shouldn't try to create "cool" Web pages. Yes, by all means, do so. This is a brand new medium and pushing its design limits is a big part of the fun, and a great way to learn.

Above all, use the power of hypertext to clarify your information. Hypertext allows you to serve content to your readers in simple chunks; the hypertext structure reveals additional relationships in the information and allows your readers to choose a level of complexity suitable to their own needs. You can't assume that all your readers have the same high level of sophistication and comprehension you have. As a statistician friend of mine is fond of saying, "Only half of us are smarter than average."

The Internet—and the Web in particular—is growing so fast that many Internet experts are worried that bandwidth (essentially the network's capacity to handle traffic) is starting to get scarce. So it's considered polite practice (good netiquette) to keep to a minimum the amount of data you're asking others to move across their networks on your behalf. Large graphic elements and long sound samples eat up bandwidth. Such objects should not be forced on readers without their informed consent. One approach commonly found on the Web is to use a small version of a graphic, often called a thumbnail, as a link to a larger version. For example, this bit of HTML

```
Click <A HREF="Large_AE.GIF"> Albert
<IMG SRC="Small_AE.GIF" ALT="Einstein" ALIGN=middle></A>
to see a large (90K bytes) picture of the scientist.
```

creates the display shown in Figure 3.1.

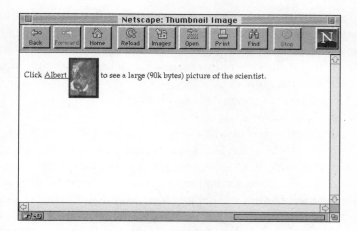

Figure 3.1: Using a thumbnail to access a larger image

The relative URL addressing (using a partial URL to refer to the location of a file relative to the URL of the current page) used in the HTML for Figure 3.1 requires that the two image files referenced in the HTML anchors—Large_AE.GIF and Small_AE.GIF—must be in the same directory as the Web page containing the links. The name Albert and the small image are together the anchor of a link to the larger image file, Large_AE.GIF. Clicking either one will fetch the larger file and pass it to a helper application (or to your browser itself if you are using it as an image viewer) to display it in a separate window as an external image. By telling readers in the text how large the image file is, you provide them with the information needed to estimate how long it will take to download the image. Note the use of the ALT attribute in the IMG tag to direct nongraphical browsers to display the text "Click Albert Einstein to see a large (90K bytes) picture of the scientist."

GENERAL PRINCIPLE NUMBER TWO

Good work is never done. It is not until after your information is made available on the Web that you'll begin to understand what it was you wanted in the first place. You should expect to frequently update and revise much of the work you put on the Web. As you add to and expand the information on a page, you'll have the opportunity to work with its structure, improve its looks, and replace any dead URLs—links to Web pages or servers that no longer exist. You'll also have the benefit of feedback from other people who have read your work. It's a good idea—in fact it's an accepted Web convention—to include your signature and e-mail address on your work. And don't be embarrassed to ask your readers for comments.

A decade ago, a speaker at a computer language conference I attended formulated this principle into the following law which he named after himself. Herewith is Biddlestone's law:

The requirements of any system are a function of the experience gained installing that system for the user.

One thing this implies is that whatever information you have, just go ahead and mark it up into a Web page. Don't spend a lot of time planning out the design: Just take the content in whatever state it's in, do a simple markup, check it out with your favorite browser, and upload it to your server. Now you can really look at it, and test the links to explore how your page fits in the context of the Webspace and the Web at large. Many pages on the World Wide Web are "Under construction" or "Work in progress." You should not be ashamed to place unfinished or even unverified information on your Web pages, as long as you inform your readers of the situation.

GENERAL PRINCIPLE NUMBER THREE
Have fun :-)

APPROACHES TO WRITING WEB PAGES

The way you approach creating a hypertext work for the World Wide Web depends on what kind of information you want to serve and how much of it is already in digital form. Broadly speaking, there are two approaches: top-down and bottom-up. If you are starting a work from scratch and there is little or no existing information already available in digital form, then work from the top down. If there is already a lot of information available that needs organizing, or if there's an existing work to be converted to hypertext, then start from the bottom and work your way up. Of course, not all hypertext applications fall easily into one of these two categories. Most real-world projects are a combination of new work and existing material. This is typical of organizations that already make use of electronically distributed information.

A third approach you might find useful is stealing. Well, borrowing anyway—if you find something you like, figure out how the author did it and copy it. You may prefer to think of this as borrowing ideas; if so, you should pay back the ideas with interest. Please—only copy the structure and the hypertext links to other, external Web sites, not the content from somebody else's Web page. You don't want a Webspace that's a "look and feel" clone of someone else's either, so don't copy background patterns or distinctive icons. Avoid copying anything from pages that have explicit copyright or trademark statements. When in doubt, ask for permission. And give credit where it's due.

Once you've decided on your approach and have put up a few pages to test out your design ideas, take some time to plan out the entire Webspace. Even a Webspace centered on a personal home page can quickly grow to encompass three or four dozen files. The mapping of the connection between conceptual areas of a Webspace and the physical layout of directories and files can be critical to its maintenance and growth. Figure out which pages will reside at the root of the Webspace and which will be in subdirectories. Putting images in their own subdirectories is a good idea. Those images that are used in common across several pages should be in a subdirectory at the root. Same with sounds, binaries, and other multimedia files.

Many Web servers use a default filename such as index.html for the home page of a Webspace, or Webspace subdirectory if none is provided in an URL. Take advantage of this default to shorten the URLs of the main entry points into your Webspace. For example, my Webspace is on my current Internet Service provider's system under my userid, laronson. My file, *index.html,* is a simple annotated listing with links to the principal pages, with my personal homepage, *homepage.html,* listed first. On my business card, I list my URL as:

```
http://www.interport.net/~laronson/
```

Consider also placing a file at the root and in each subdirectory of the Webspace with a file name such as *index.txt.* Use this file as a database of information about the Webspace or subdirectory. Include the file name and title of each Web page, the author(s) of the page, creation and update dates, lists of the images used on the page, and whatever else you and others might need to maintain that Webspace. The advantage of using a text file is that you can maintain the indexes to the Webspace with the same editor you use to write the Web pages.

Good HTML Style

As the Web continues to grow, it becomes more important to write HTML that conforms to certain guidelines and styles. Right now there are dozens of different Web browsers available. The major online services provide Web browsers as part of their offerings and current releases of the most popular operating systems (UNIX, Microsoft Windows 95, Macintosh System 7.5, and OS/2 Warp) have built-in Internet connectivity. The growth of the Web user community shows no sign of slowing. It's important to write HTML that will look good on any client, now and in the future, not just on Netscape and the current generation of browsers.

This section will offer some guidelines as to the dos and don'ts of writing good HTML documents: pages that are easy to maintain and will produce presentable results on any browser. Bear in mind that there's no authority that dictates what is and what isn't good HTML style. These guidelines reflect the lessons learned by many Web authors, that is, the many authors who share their experiences using newsgroups and mailing lists. Check Appendix B for listings of these resources and make it a practice to regularly visit them. The Web is still in its infancy and no one knows what it will grow into.

It is a good idea to sign and date all pages you put on the Web so that your readers can form some impression of the authority of the page—how recent it is and how reliable the source of the information is. On a home page or any page that serves as an introduction to a hypertext work, your signature should include your full name and e-mail address so readers can send you comments on your work. You can make a link from your name back to your personal home page. On less important pages of the work, your signature can just be your initials linked back to the authorship information on the home page. When developing a new Webspace, it's a good idea to put the URL of each page at the bottom so that printed versions of the pages are readily identifiable. Later, when the pages are more stable, the identifying URL can be commented out.

Remember that your documents are going on a World Wide Web, so when writing dates, use a long format with the name of the month spelled out or abbreviated—in other words, July 4, 1995, or 4-Jul-95. Formats such as 7/4/95 can be ambiguous in some cultures. The same holds true for monetary amounts. Other countries such as Canada and Australia use the dollar sign. Make it clear which currency you mean by writing US$19.95 or $19.95 USD, for example, instead of just $19.95.

COMMON MISTAKES

Probably the most prevalent kind of error in writing HTML is the misuse of paragraph breaks. In part this comes from working so much with one browser that you begin to accept its handling of white space as common. It also comes from the syntax change from an empty paragraph tag in HTML2 to a container in HTML3. Since HTML3 is backwards compatible with HTML2, you can use either form. In either case, avoid the temptation to adjust the spacing

of page elements by placing extra paragraph tags where none is necessary—
around headings, lists, blockquotes, or address blocks, for example.

Trust the readers' browsers and forget about making such "adjustments" to
the layout. You'll be better off. Because it's cleaner, I recommend using the
HTML3 container form of the paragraph element, especially when including
an attribute. For example:

```
<H3 ALIGN=center>WWW Menu Specials</H3>
<P ALIGN=center>
Hong Kong Flu<BR>
Beijing Duck<BR>
Turkish Taffy<BR>
French Farce
</P>
```

to create the centered menu effect of Figure 3.2.

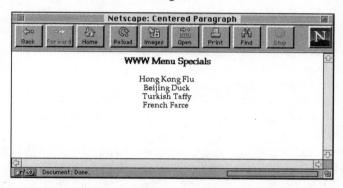

Figure 3.2: A centered paragraph

A common source of error is not properly closing an HTML element. With
character entities this means forgetting the trailing semicolon or having blanks
separate the character entity from the rest of the text. A level 2 heading introducing your professional experience should be written without space as:

```
<H2>R&eacute;sum&eacute;</H2>
```

Don't take a shortcut and write:

```
<H2>Resume</H2>
```

which is just encouragement to continue. It's also easy to forget that the
ampersand is the escape character. Make sure you write AT&T and not

AT&T. Forgetting one of the double quote marks that should enclose an URL is also a common error. Some browsers don't care if an URL is in quotes, but many do, and most will have a problem if one quotation mark is there and the other isn't. To be absolutely correct, all attribute values should be in quotes. It's become a general practice, however, to omit the quotes if the attribute value is a simple number or constant, such as in this image tag:

```
<IMG SRC="images/boop.gif" ALIGN=top BORDER=2>
```

With tag elements, errors can occur when the closing right angle bracket (>) is missing. Many browsers will properly render strings that contain a single right angle bracket with no matching left bracket (<) as if that character were part of the text. For example, <This is not a tag> will be displayed as: <This is not a tag>. However, it is recommended that the character entity > be used for the right angle bracket—<This is not a tag>—because if there are any other tag errors in the document, having an extra > around will only make matters worse. With containers, forgetting the slash (/) that begins the ending element will cause errors, as will having blanks on either side of the slash. Browsers are very forgiving. In most cases, they will ignore an incorrect ending tag and continue applying whatever tag was in effect to the following text, possibly to the end of the page.

The nesting of tags should be done carefully. As a general rule, tags that define styles should be inside of tags that create structure. Without enumerating all the possible combinations, here are a few guidelines.

Avoid nesting other tags inside of a heading. The exceptions to this rule are the line break tag, <BR>, image tags, and anchors marking the heading as a hypertext link. Headings should never contain any tags that imply paragraph breaks. This includes other headings, paragraph tags, horizontal rules, list structures, blockquotes, addresses, tables, and preformatted style tags. If you want to create a multiple line heading, use the line break tag <BR>. Likewise, headings should never be used inside tags other than <FORM></FORM>, <TABLE></TABLE> and <DL></DL>, and, of course, the <BODY></BODY> and <HTML></HTML> tags that define the document. Enclosing headings within any other tags doesn't make sense, and the results are unpredictable.

The use of style tags to change the rendering of a heading should be avoided except when applied to a small part of the heading text, for example:

```
<H3>Some <STRONG>Important</STRONG> phone numbers</H3>
```

Image tags can be used inside of a heading to provide a graphic aligned to the heading text. The key to understanding the behavior of inline images in a heading, or anywhere on a page, for that matter, is in the word "inline." That is, an image is just like a big fat character in a line of text. It moves and word-wraps with the text. There are no implied paragraph breaks, line breaks or even word breaks separating the image from the text unless you explicitly supply them with paragraph tags, line break tags or spaces.

If you want to create the effect of a button bar as in the illustration below, the images tags defining the buttons must be specified without spaces between the tags:

```
<A HREF="top.html"><IMG SRC="top.gif" BORDER=0 ALT="[TOP]"></A><A
HREF="page3.html"><IMG SRC="prev.gif" BORDER=0 ALT="[PREV]"></A><A
HREF="page5.html"><IMG SRC="next.gif" BORDER=0 ALT="[NEXT]"></A>
```

Placing the image tags one per line in your HTML source:

```
<A HREF="top.html"><IMG SRC="top.gif" BORDER=0 ALT="[TOP]"></A>
<A HREF="page3.html"><IMG SRC="prev.gif" BORDER=0 ALT="[PREV]"></A>
<A HREF="page5.html"><IMG SRC="next.gif" BORDER=0 ALT="[NEXT]"></A>
```

may look neater, especially if each image is enclosed in an anchor tag, but the browser will interpret the carriage returns as word breaks and insert spaces between the buttons.

Most of the time you can write HTML without worrying about how you lay out your tags and content, but as you see, you have to be a little more careful around anchors. Many authors unwittingly create anchors with "tails." For example, this may look reasonable:

```
<H2>Netscape Navigator
<A HREF="http://www.netscape.com/">
<IMG SRC="NN_logo.gif">
</A>
</H2>
```

but, as seen in Figure 3.3, the blue underscoring marking the anchor extends one space beyond the image. It comes from the carriage return in the HTML text after the image tag but before the close of the anchor with </A>. Most browsers will remove a leading blank following an actual or implied paragraph break, but the trailing word break that is put in place of the carriage return is kept as part of the anchor.

Figure 3.3: An anchor with a tail

It would have been better to write the HTML:

```
<H2>Netscape Navigator
<A HREF="http://www.netscape.com/"><IMG SRC="NN_logo.gif"></A>
</H2>
```

One last point with regard to tags is that if you are copying elements from other pages on the Web, avoid using any obsolete elements (tags that were in earlier versions of HTML but are now superseded by other HTML3 elements). These obsolete elements include <PLAINTEXT></PLAINTEXT>, <XMP></XMP>, <LISTING></LISTING>, <HPx></HPx>, and <COMMENT></COMMENT>. The first three should be replaced with the preformatted tags <PRE></PRE>; <HP></HP> (highlighted phrase) should be replaced with appropriate style tags; and <COMMENT></COMMENT> should be replaced with SGML comments which are enclosed by the strings <!-- and -->.

HTML3 browsers will accept most HTML2 tags. There are a few tags, however, that have fallen out of use. They are not recommended for use in new documents and few browsers will render them distinctively. These include the list forms, <DIR></DIR> and <MENU></MENU>, some style tags, such as <CODE></CODE> and <KBD></KBD>, and some Netscape extensions such as <BLINK></BLINK>.

URL errors are a different matter. An URL error won't affect the rendering of the page in a browser's display, but a badly composed URL will be incorrectly interpreted and you'll get an unknown server error or a file not found error. Relative URLs have strong advantages—they're shorter and they make a collection of documents portable. However, relative URLs should be used with care, since the URL does not contain all the information necessary to construct the link. The missing server and path information is taken by the browser from the URL of the document that contains the link. What is always safe is a relative reference to a file in the same directory as the current page. Files in a subdirectory can be safely referenced by using slash—a forward slash (/), not the backslash (\) used in DOS path names—as in:

```
our clerk, <A HREF="accounting/Cratchet.html">Bob Cratchet</A>
```

Refer to the parent directory of the directory containing the current page by using two dots (..). However, this may not work with a parent directory of a parent directory, as in:

```
<A HREF="../../officers/Scrooge.html">my boss</A>
```

A single dot refers to the current directory, thus,

```
<A HREF="./accounting/Cratchet.html">Bob Cratchet</A>
```

is the same as:

```
<A HREF="accounting/Cratchet.html">Bob Cratchet</A>
```

An URL beginning with a single slash (/) is the entire path, including the name of the drive, to the file:

```
<A HREF="/staff/accounting/Cratchet.html">Bob Cratchet</A>
```

Most browsers will let you set the default home page URL. If you are not permanently connected to the Internet, it's a good idea to set this to a file on your own machine using the "file:" URL method. On a Windows system for example; an URL pointing to the index file in the local copy of your Webspace on your C drive might look something like this:

```
file:///C:/WINDOWS/WWW/HTML/INDEX.HTM
```

Notice the three forward slashes after "file:". Since this a local file, there is no server name or IP number after the first two slashes. The third slash is necessary to show that the path begins at the root. The hard drive designation "C:" is considered a subdirectory of the root. The rest of the URL must point to an actual file since there is no server running to establish a default.

Note: Netscape Navigator and some other browsers will provide an ftp-style directory listing if the URL ends in a directory name. This feature is useful for development and maintenance. This feature is also the default action of some servers if no file with the proper default name (index.html) is found, so it's a good idea to have a file with the default name in your Webspace. Even if you never link to it, it prevents readers from "ftp fishing" through your files.

Finally, be aware of the different file naming conventions. DOS, Windows 3.1, and Windows NT have the most restrictive scheme—up to eight characters for the file name plus a three-character extension. Most Web servers are UNIX based where file names can be up to 255 characters and contain any character except the forward slash used to separate directories. Macintosh file names can be up to 31 characters in length, cannot contain a colon (:), and are not case sensitive. UNIX file names are sensitive to case, so a link that works locally on your Macintosh may not be valid when the files are moved to a UNIX server because of capitalization errors.

The best advice is not to mix cases in your file and directory names, keep them eight characters or less in length (or at least unique within the first eight characters), and don't use any characters other than letters, numbers, the dot (.) and the underscore (_). Although other characters in a file name will probably not cause problems, if you must have them, it's a good idea to code them in hexadecimal notation using the percent character (%) followed by two hexadecimal digits. For example, this link to the file, "r&d rept.txt":

```
<A HREF="r%26d%2-rept.txt">Research and Development</A>
```

uses the sequence "%26" for the ampersand and "%20" for the space character. Check the back of your modem manual; there's probably an ASCII reference chart there that you can use to look up the hexadecimal equivalents for special characters.

These are only some of the more common sources of error. Developing a good HTML style is a matter of practice, studying the work of others, and finally, good common sense.

Tutorials

This chapter contains three "walk throughs" of creating Web pages using the HTML elements and techniques in the last two chapters. The first is the creation of a simple personal home page. The second is a guest book page with an interactive form. The third is the conversion of a word processing document into a hypertext work. These three exercises cover much of what's involved in building a Webspace. The HTML used is basic enough to produce excellent results over a wide range of HTML2 and HTML3 browsers.

CREATING A HOME PAGE

A home page is the hypertext document within a work that is intended as the primary starting point of the work. This is where the work is introduced and placed in the larger context of the Web in which it's contained. Your personal home page is the starting point for a hypertext work about you. Since it will be created from scratch, I recommend using a top-down approach, starting with a simple outline like this:

1 Your name

2 A welcome message

3 Information about you

4 A statement of your goals

5 Current activities/announcements

6 Related information

7 Signature, address, time stamps

You needn't follow the above outline exactly in creating your own home page, but this is the information readers generally expect to see. The information under each heading will be summary in nature; the details will be in other, hyperlinked pages.

Before we begin editing the HTML files we need somewhere to put them. Create a new directory for these files. This directory will be the local, working copy of the Webspace. Figure 4.4 refers to this directory as WWW. Into this new directory place a text file containing an HTML template. Give this file an obvious file name such as *template.html* and save it write-protected or as a stationary document to prevent accidentally overwriting it. Make sure it's saved as a plain text file instead of in your word processor's normal format.

Next we'll take a copy of the template file and fill in the TITLE and BODY sections based on the outline above. For this example home page, let's use the seventeenth century astronomer Johannes Kepler. For the content, I used as a reference Arthur Koestler's book *The Sleepwalkers*:

```
<HTML>
<!-- Kepler's Home Page, created 1 August, AD 1610 -->
<HEAD>
<TITLE>Kepler's Home Page</TITLE>
</HEAD>
<BODY>
<H1>Johannes Kepler</H1>
<EM>Welcome to my Homepage!</EM>
<HR>
<H2>Who am I</H2>
<H2>What is this Document</H2>
<H2>Current Activities</H2>
<H2>Related Information</H2>
<HR>
<ADDRESS>
Johannes Kepler &lt;kepler@astronova.com&gt;<BR>
Last updated: September 7, 1610
</ADDRESS>
</BODY>
</HTML>
```

Edit and save this file in your WWW directory as *homepage.html*. All HTML documents should have file names that end with the extension ".html" unless the files will reside on a system that only allows three-character extensions, in which case they should have the extension ".htm." Opened in a browser, you'll see a display similar to that of Figure 4.1.

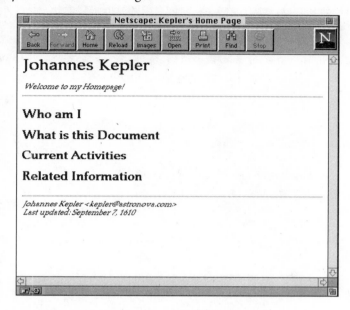

Figure 4.1: Johannes Kepler's home page—first draft

The next step is filling in paragraphs of narrative text under each heading. We'll put in the hypertext links in a later stage, when the page and its content are more stable. Under the first two headings, just a couple of plain paragraphs will do. "Current Activities" will be a list of items and descriptions, so a definition list will be used. Under "Related Information" will be an unordered list of other World Wide Web and Internet sites. The HTML should now look something like:

```
<HTML>
<!-- Kepler's Home Page, created 1 August, AD 1610 -->
<HEAD>
<TITLE>Johannes Kepler's Home Page</TITLE>
</HEAD>
<BODY>
<H1>Johannes Kepler</H1>
<EM>Welcome to my Home page!</EM>
```

```
<HR>
<H2>Who am I</H2>
<P>I am an Author and Astronomer; servant and successor to the great
Tycho Brahe. Currently employed as Imperial Mathematician to his
highness, Emperor Rudolph II.</P>
<H2>What is this Document</H2>
<P>This is my home page on the World Wide Web with which I endeavor to
provide the World with the latest and most important news from the
frontiers of Astronomy.</P>
<H2>Current Activities</H2>
<P>Much has happened the past few months.
 Here are some of the highlights.</P>
<DL>
<DT><H3><CITE>A New Astronomy</CITE></H3></DT>
<DD>Based A PHYSICS OF THE SKY derived from
Investigations of the MOTIONS OF THE STAR MARS Founded on
Observations of the noble Tycho Brahe. The mystery of planetary
motion has been solved, revealing The Creator's grand design.
<P>
After 8 hard years of work, my opus is finally in print.
You can order <CITE>Astro Nova</CITE> here. If all goes well,
I'll have a hypertext version available shortly
</DD>
<DT><H3>Jupiter has Moons! Saturn has Ears!</H3></DT>
<DD>Galileo's astonishing new discoveries resulting from his
investigations of the heavenly bodies as described in his
booklet, <CITE>Messenger from the Stars</CITE>.</DD>
<DT><H3>The Telescope</H3></DT>
<DD>Everybody is talking about what may be the most important
invention of our age. Thanks to the generosity of our noble
patron, the Duke of Bavaria, we now have access to one of these
amazing devices. Read our draft report on Jupiter's four
wandering satellites.</DD>
</DL>
<H2>Related Information</H2>
<UL>
<LI>The Tycho Brahe Memorial Page
<LI>Welcome to Prague
<LI>Galileo's World of Wonders
```

```
<LI>Yahoo's Astronomy Index
</UL>
<HR>
<P>This page, dear reader, is <EM>Under Construction</EM> so please be
patient. Your comments and suggestions are welcome. Please send them to
the address below.</P>
<HR>
<ADDRESS>
Johannes Kepler &lt;kepler@astronova.com&gt;<BR>
Last updated: September 7, 1610
</ADDRESS>
</BODY>
</HTML>
```

which, opened in Netscape, appears as Figure 4.2

Figure 4.2: Johannes Kepler's home page—second draft

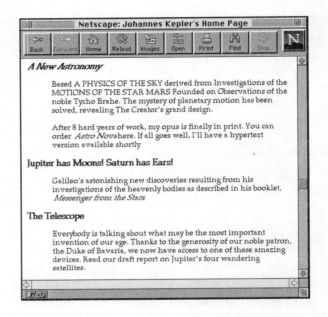

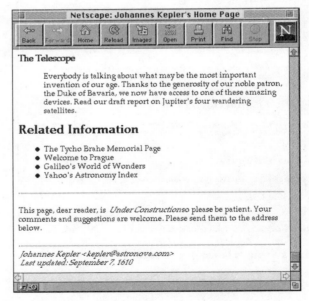

Figure 4.2: Johannes Kepler's home page—second draft (continued)

Okay so far. Let's add an image to the welcome message. There are many ways to get a picture onto your computer—scanner, digital camera, or Photo CD, to name a few—and the image file formats differ from one operating system to the next. Digitized images must be converted into the GIF format before they can be used inline on a page.(Inline JPEG images are also accepted by some, but not all, browsers). There are utilities (many shareware or freeware) that can be used to convert images from one format to another. See Appendix B.

The image tag will go before the emphasis style tag. It could just as well be inside of the emphasis tags, since images cannot be styled.

```
<H1>Johannes Kepler</H1>
<IMG SRC="images/kepler.gif">
<EM>Welcome to my Homepage!</EM>
<HR>
```

The carriage return after the image tag will force a blank between the image and the text. This looks better than having the image right up against the text. This is okay, but let's go a step further and force the text to flow around the image by adding the ALIGN attribute to the image tag. We'll incorporate the level 1 heading and use the HSPACE attribute for better positioning.

```
<IMG SRC="images/kepler.gif" ALIGN=left HSPACE=16>
<H1>Johannes Kepler</H1>
<EM>Welcome to my Homepage!</EM>
<HR CLEAR>
```

There are other alternatives. Experiment with the placement of text and images until you find something that suits you.

By now we should have a good idea where links might go. In the example above, I'll add links to the Tycho Brahe and Galileo home pages as well as to the sites listed under the "Related Information" heading (Rudolph II, unconvinced of the Web's importance, didn't have a home page. He was forced to abdicate the following year.) Links will also be added to pages on *A New Astronomy* and the Telescope. These links will use relative addressing since they refer to pages in this Webspace. See the listing below.

When you work on your home page, try to incorporate the text that anchors hypertext links into the natural flow of the paragraph's prose. Avoid using "Click here" for anchors. If a program should scan your page recording each anchor URL and its associated anchor text, "Click here" would not provide any useful information about the document it points to. Besides, you can pretty well assume that the readers know what is and what is not a link by the time they get to your page.

Here's the HTML for the next iteration of Johannes Kepler's home page. I've added small star images as bullets to the level 2 headings, fattened up the horizontal rules and indented the text paragraphs by enclosing the main part of the page in a definition list. The page, as rendered by Netscape 2.0, is shown in Figure 4.3. Figure 4.4 shows the directory structure of the Webspace.

```
<HTML>
<!-- Kepler's Home Page, created 1 August, AD 1610 -->
<HEAD>
<TITLE>Johannes Kepler's Home Page</TITLE>
</HEAD>
<BODY>
<IMG SRC="images/kepler.gif" ALIGN=left HSPACE=16>
<H1>Johannes Kepler</H1>
<EM>Welcome to my Homepage!</EM>
<BR CLEAR=left>
<HR SIZE=4>
<DL>
<DT><H2><IMG SRC="images/redstar.gif"> Who am I</H2></DT>
<DD>I am an Author and Astronomer; servant and successor to the great
Tycho Brahe. Currently employed as Imperial Mathematician to his
highness, Emperor Rudolph II.
</DD>
<DT><H2><IMG SRC="images/redstar.gif"> What is this Document</H2></DT>
<DD>This is my homepage on the
<A HREP="http://www.w3.org/">World Wide Web</A>
with which I endeavor to provide the World with the latest and most
important news from the frontiers of Astronomy.
</DD>
<DT><H2><IMG SRC="images/redstar.gif"> Current Activities</H2></DT>
<DD>Much has happened the past few months.
 Here are some of the highlights.
<DL>
<DT><H3>
<A HREF="newastro.html"><CITE>A New Astronomy</CITE></A>
</H3></DT>
<DD>Based A PHYSICS OF THE SKY derived from
Investigations of the MOTIONS OF THE STAR MARS Founded on
Observations of the noble Tycho Brahe. The mystery of planetary
motion has been solved, finally revealing The Creator's grand
```

```
design.
<P>
After 8 hard years of work, my opus is finally in print.
You can <A HREF="order.html">order it here</A>.
If all goes well, I'll have a hypertext version of it shortly
</DD>
<DT><H3>Jupiter has Moons! Saturn has Ears!</H3></DT>
<DD>Galileo's astonishing new discoveries resulting from his
investigations of the heavenly bodies as described in his
booklet, <CITE>Messenger from the Stars</CITE>.</DD>
<DT><H3><A HREF="telescope.html">The Telescope</A></H3></DT>
<DD>Everybody is talking about what may be the most important
invention of our age. Thanks to the generosity of our noble
patron, the Duke of Bavaria, we now have access to one of these
amazing devices. Read our <A HREF="jupiter.html">draft report
on Jupiter's four wandering satellites</A>.</DD>
</DL>
</DD>
<DT><H2><IMG SRC="images/redstar.gif"> Related Information</H2></DT>
<DD><UL>
<LI><A HREF="http://www.nada.kth.se/~fred/tycho.html">
The Tycho Brahe Memorial Page</A>
<LI><A HREF="http://turnpike.net/metro/muselik/prague.html">
Welcome to Prague</A>
<LI><A HREF="http://www-groups.dcs.st-
and.ac.uk/~history/Mathematicians/Galileo.html">
Galileo's World of Wonders</A>
<LI><A HREF="http://www.yahoo.com/Science/Astronomy/">
Yahoo's Astronomy Index</A>
</UL>
</DD>
</DL>
<HR SIZE=2>
<P><IMG SRC="images/workman.gif"> This page, dear reader, is <EM>Under
Construction</EM> so please be patient. Your comments and suggestions
are welcome. Please send them to the address below.</P>
<HR SIZE=4>
<ADDRESS>
Johannes Kepler
```

```
&lt;<A HREF="mailto:kepler@nova.com">jkepler@astronova.com</A>&gt;<BR>
Last updated: September 7, 1610
</ADDRESS>
</BODY>
</HTML>
```

Johannes Kepler

Welcome to my Homepage!

★ Who am I

I am an Author and Astronomer; servant and successor to the great Tycho Brahe. Currently employed as Imperial Mathematician to his highness, Emperor Rudolph II.

★ What is this Document

This is my homepage on the World Wide Web with which I endeavor to provide the World with the latest and most important news from the frontiers of Astronomy.

★ Current Activities

Much has happened the past few months. Here are some of the highlights.

A New Astronomy

Based A PHYSICS OF THE SKY derived from Investigations of the MOTIONS OF THE STAR MARS Founded on Observations of the noble Tycho Brahe. The mystery of planetary motion has been solved, finally revealing The Creator's grand design.

After 8 hard years of work, my opus is finally in print. You can order it here. If all goes well, I'll have a hypertext version of it shortly

Jupiter has Moons! Saturn has Ears!

Galileo's astonishing new discoveries resulting from his investigations of the heavenly bodies as described in his booklet, *Messenger from the Stars*.

The Telescope

Everybody is talking about what may be the most important invention of our age. Thanks to the generosity of our noble patron, the Duke of Bavaria, we now have access to one of these amazing devices. Read our draft report on Jupiter's four wandering satellites.

★ Related Information

- The Tycho Brahe Memorial Page
- Welcome to Prague
- Galileo's World of Wonders
- Yahoo's Astronomy Index

This page, dear reader, is *Under Construction*, so please be patient. Your comments and suggestions are welcome. Please send them to the address below.

Johannes Kepler <jkepler@astronova.com>
Last updated: September 7, 1610

Figure 4.3: Johannes Kepler's home page—final draft

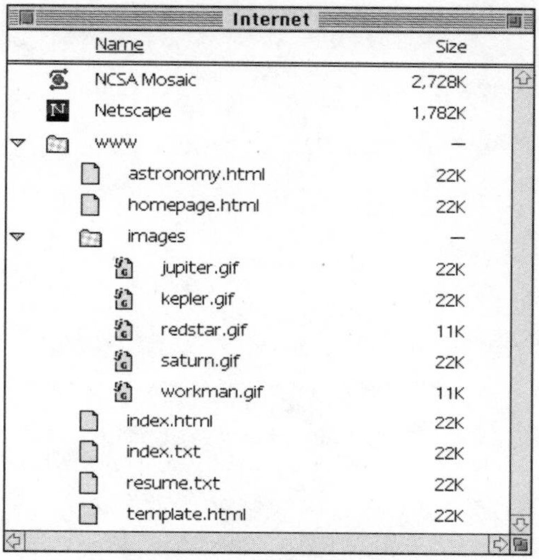

```
┌──────────────────────── Internet ════════════════════════┐
│          Name                            Size              │
├──────────────────────────────────────────────────────────┤
│    ☎  NCSA Mosaic                       2,728K            │
│    Ⓝ  Netscape                          1,782K            │
│ ▽ 🗀  www                                  —               │
│         📄  astronomy.html                 22K            │
│         📄  homepage.html                  22K            │
│ ▽      🗀  images                           —             │
│            📄  jupiter.gif                 22K            │
│            📄  kepler.gif                  22K            │
│            📄  redstar.gif                 11K            │
│            📄  saturn.gif                  22K            │
│            📄  workman.gif                 11K            │
│      📄  index.html                        22K            │
│      📄  index.txt                         22K            │
│      📄  resume.txt                        22K            │
│      📄  template.html                     22K            │
└──────────────────────────────────────────────────────────┘
```

Figure 4.4: Directory structure of a simple Webspace

CREATING A GUEST BOOK—A FORM APPLICATION

The World Wide Web is a client-server environment. And that means interactivity. The simplest way to interact with your readers through a Web page is with a form that electronically mails readers' input back to you. This method is a one-shot deal. Your server sends the form to the reader, who fills in information and sends it off to you. Other, more interactive methods of exchanging information with your readers require a script—a computer program running either on the server or an applet downloaded to the reader's browser.

The form application developed here is a simple guest book page that will allow visitors to let you know of their visits to your Webspace. The information is sent back to you via e-mail messages from which you extract information to be added to a visitors' page. Sooner or later you'll develop a cgi script to process the information in real time. All that you'll have to do then is change the value of the ACTION attribute to the URL of the script.

The form will ask the reader for his or her name, e-mail address, location, and home page URL. The reader will be able to rate the Webspace and leave a comment. Submit and Reset buttons will be at the bottom of the page. Figure 4.6 shows the final version of the page.

Using comments, here's the basic layout of the page:

```
<HTML>
<!-- Guest Book from "HTML3 Manual of Style"  -->
<!-- Larry Aronson, October 10, 1995          -->
<HEAD>
<TITLE>Guest Book</TITLE>
</HEAD>
<BODY>
<H1>Guest Book</H1>
<!-- WELCOME MESSAGE -->
<HR SIZE=4>

<FORM METHOD=POST ACTION="mailto:yew@yerplace.com">
<H3>About You</H3>
<!-- FIELDS FOR name, email, location, url -->
<HR>
<H3>Your Opinion</H3>
<!-- RADIO BUTTON SET OF CHOICES -->
<HR>
<H3>Comments</H3>
<!-- TEXTAREA FOR COMMENTS -->
<HR>
<!-- SUBMIT AND RESET BUTTONS -->
</FORM>

<!-- ADDRESS AND EXIT LINKS -->
</BODY>
</HTML>
```

The beginning FORM tag,

```
<FORM METHOD=POST ACTION="mailto:yew@yerplace.com">
```

is placed just after the welcome message. It could go just after the BODY tag; it makes no difference, as long as it appears before the tags defining the form's input objects. The ACTION attribute specifies that the contents of the form should be e-mailed to the fictitious address, yew@yerplace.com.

The first section, *About You,* will have four sets of prompts and input fields; one set per line. Each input field will be 40 characters wide (most browsers will let the reader enter more characters than the fixed width of the field.) We'll give the fields obvious names.

```
<H3>About You</H3>
<!-- FIELDS FOR name, email, location, url -->
<P>Your Name: <INPUT TYPE="text" NAME="nam" SIZE=40><BR>
Email Address: <INPUT TYPE="text" NAME="addr" SIZE=40><BR>
Location: <INPUT TYPE="text" NAME="loc" SIZE=40><BR>
Home Page URL: <INPUT TYPE="text" NAME="url" SIZE=40></P>
<HR>
```

Figure 4.5 shows how these fields would appear in a typical browser.

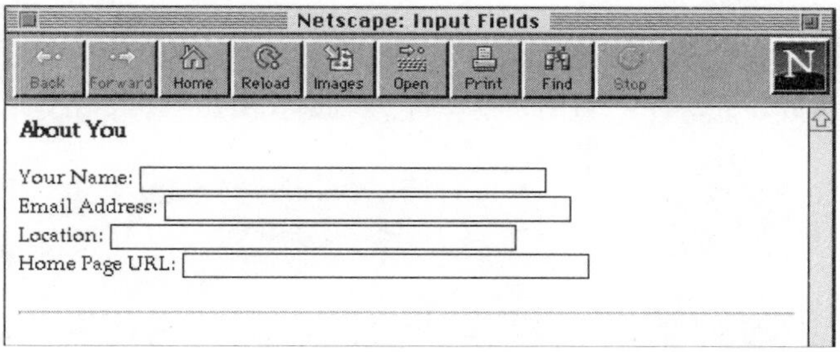

Figure 4.5: Input fields

Wouldn't it be nice if the prompts and input fields could be aligned vertically? Well, we can do that by putting the prompts and input fields in a 4-row by 2-column table, like so:

```
<H3>About You</H3>
<!-- FIELDS FOR name, email, location, url -->
<TABLE>
<TR><TD>Your Name:</TD>
    <TD><INPUT TYPE="text" NAME="nam" SIZE=40></TD></TR><BR>
<TR><TD>E-mail Address:</TD>
    <TD><INPUT TYPE="text" NAME="addr" SIZE=40></TD></TR><BR>
<TR><TD>State or Country:</TD>
    <TD><INPUT TYPE="text" NAME="loc" SIZE=40></TD></TR><BR>
<TR><TD>Home Page URL:</TD>
    <TD><INPUT TYPE="text" NAME="url" SIZE=40></TD></TR><BR>
</TABLE>
<HR>
```

The default table attributes do just fine here, illustrating the power of tables to organize content. Note that we've dropped the paragraph tags but kept the line break tags, <BR>, just in case someone out there has a browser that supports forms but not tables.

The radio buttons in the next section are straightforward. We will bind them into a set by giving each the same name, "choice." The VALUE attributes are given numeric values from 1 to 4 so that when the reader clicks the submit button, one of these numbers will be returned, depending on which radio button is selected. For example, if the reader selects the radio button labeled "Just OK," the form will return "choice=2."

```
<H3>Your Opinion</H3>
<!-- RADIO BUTTON SET OF CHOICES -->
<P><INPUT TYPE="radio" NAME="choice" VALUE=4> Hotlist Pick!<BR>
   <INPUT TYPE="radio" NAME="choice" VALUE=3 CHECKED> Very
Good<BR>
   <INPUT TYPE="radio" NAME="choice" VALUE=2> Just OK<BR>
   <INPUT TYPE="radio" NAME="choice" VALUE=1> Trash</P>
<HR>
```

The comments field is the easiest. We'll encourage our readers by providing a large 12-row-by 60-character field.

```
<TEXTAREA NAME="comment" ROWS=12 COLS=60></TEXTAREA>
```

Be aware that the above is not the same as:

```
<TEXTAREA NAME="comment" ROWS=12 COLS=60>
</TEXTAREA>
```

The latter initializes the input field with a single blank. I point this out because the difference between no input, single blank input, and all blank input is one of those things that give programmers headaches.

Finally our Submit and Reset buttons. It's a good idea to explicitly provide the button labels using the VALUE attribute.

```
<!-- SUBMIT AND RESET BUTTONS -->
<P>Click one:
<INPUT TYPE="submit" VALUE="Send It">
<INPUT TYPE="reset" VALUE="Forget It"></P>
```

With a bit of narrative text to guide the reader along, here's the complete contents of the file, guestbook.html. Figure 4.6 shows it rendered by a typical browser.

```
<HTML>
<!-- Guest Book from "HTML3 Manual of Style"  -->
<!-- Larry Aronson, October 10, 1995          -->
<HEAD>
<TITLE>Guest Book</TITLE>
</HEAD>
<H1>Guest Book</H1>
<!-- WELCOME MESSAGE -->
Hi, Welcome to my <STRONG>Guest Book</STRONG>.
<P>Here you can leave information to let me know of your visit to my
Webspace. Check the <A HREF="visitors.html">visitor's page</A> in a day
or two for your info.</P>
<HR SIZE=4>
<FORM METHOD=POST ACTION="mailto:yeruserid@yerplace.com">
<H3>About You</H3>
<!-- FIELDS FOR name, email, location, url -->
<TABLE>
<TR><TD>Your Name:</TD>
<TD><INPUT TYPE="text" NAME="nam" SIZE="40"></TD></TR><BR>
<TR><TD>E-mail Address:</TD>
<TD><INPUT TYPE="text" NAME="addr" SIZE="40"></TD></TR><BR>
<TR><TD>Location:</TD>
<TD><INPUT TYPE="text" NAME="loc" SIZE="40"></TD></TR><BR>
<TR><TD>Home Page URL:</TD>
<TD><INPUT TYPE="text" NAME="url" SIZE="40"></TD></TR><BR>
</TABLE>
<HR>
<H3>Your Opinion</H3>
<!-- RADIO BUTTON SET OF CHOICES -->
<P>Please let me know what you think of my Webspace.</P>
<P><INPUT TYPE="radio" NAME="choice" VALUE=4> Hotlist Pick!<BR>
<INPUT TYPE="radio" NAME="choice" VALUE=3 CHECKED> Very Good<BR>
<INPUT TYPE="radio" NAME="choice" VALUE=2> Just OK<BR>
<INPUT TYPE="radio" NAME="choice" VALUE=1> Trash</P>
<HR>
<H3>Comments</H3>
```

```
<!-- TEXTAREA FOR COMMENTS -->
<H4>Anything else you care to add? Use the input area below.</H4>
<TEXTAREA NAME="comment" ROWS=12 COLS=60></TEXTAREA>
<HR>
<!-- SUBMIT AND RESET BUTTONS -->
<P>Click one:
<INPUT TYPE="submit" VALUE="Send It">
<INPUT TYPE="reset" VALUE="Forget It"></P>
<H5>Thanks for your input.</H5>
</FORM>
<!-- ADDRESS AND EXIT LINKS -->
<H4><A HREF="homepage.html">
<IMG SRC="images/lefthand.gif" BORDER=0>
Return to my Homepage</A></H4>
<HR>
<ADDRESS>LA - 95/10/10<ADDRESS>
</BODY>
</HTML>
```

Let's suppose our net.friend, Johannes, visited our guest book filling in the fields. Clicking on the Submit button, he would have sent an e-mail message to yew@yerplace.com. with the body of that message containing:

```
nam=Johannes+Kepler&addr=jkepler@astronova.com&loc=Prague&url=http%3A%2F
%2Fwww.astronova.com%2F%7Ejkepler%2Fhomepage.html&choice=3&comment=
Looking+Good%21
```

If you put up a guest page and start getting more than one of these messages a day, you'll want a program to do all the work for you. There are a number of existing cgi scripts you can download off of the Web that, installed on your server, can do the hard work of parsing this input. In particular, I like Doug's WWW Mail Gateway. It's a PERL script that can be installed on most Web servers. It parses the input and e-mails it to a recipient, then serves a reply page of your choice back to the reader. Doug's WWW Mail Gateway requires that fields with specific names be sent to it. This can be done with hidden input fields.

To use Doug's WWW Mail Gateway (assuming our Webmaster installed it on our server) in our Guest Book, replace the FORM tag with:

```
<FORM METHOD=POST ACTION="http://www.yerplace.com/cgi-bin/mailto.pl">
```

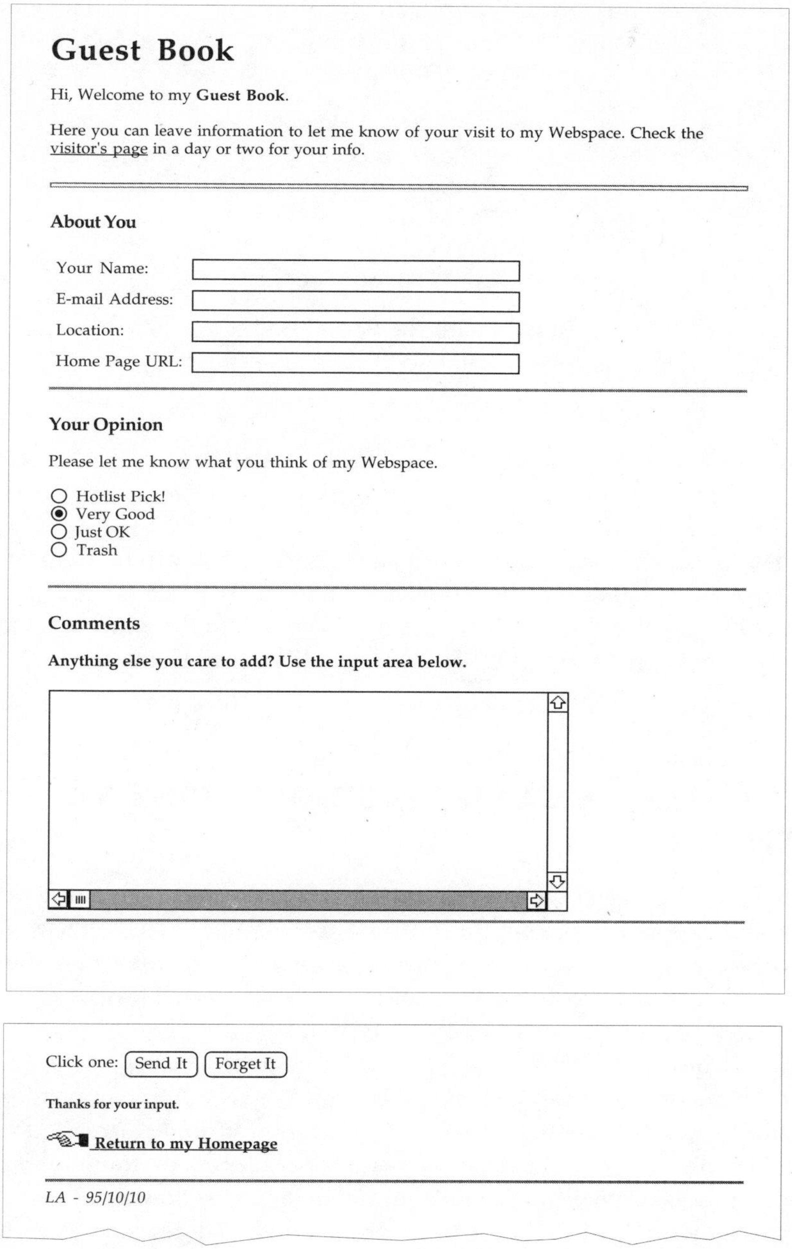

Guest Book

Hi, Welcome to my **Guest Book**.

Here you can leave information to let me know of your visit to my Webspace. Check the visitor's page in a day or two for your info.

About You

Your Name:

E-mail Address:

Location:

Home Page URL:

Your Opinion

Please let me know what you think of my Webspace.

- ○ Hotlist Pick!
- ● Very Good
- ○ Just OK
- ○ Trash

Comments

Anything else you care to add? Use the input area below.

Click one: [Send It] [Forget It]

Thanks for your input.

☞ **Return to my Homepage**

LA - 95/10/10

Figure 4.6: A guest book page

and insert the following fields to supply the required information. These input fields will be hidden; they don't appear anywhere on the Web page and the tags can be placed anywhere within the <FORM></FORM> tags.

```
<INPUT TYPE="hidden" NAME="to" VALUE="yew@yerplace.com">
<INPUT TYPE="hidden" NAME="from" VALUE="guestbook@yerplace.com">
<INPUT TYPE="hidden" NAME="name" VALUE="GuestBook Visitor">
<INPUT TYPE="hidden" NAME="sub" VALUE="Comments">
<INPUT TYPE="hidden" NAME="nexturl"
       VALUE="http://www.yerplace.com/gbreply.html">
```

The script also requires a field with the name "body." We'll change the <TEXTAREA> tag to supply this, like so.

```
<TEXTAREA NAME="body" ROWS=12 COLS=60></TEXTAREA>
```

The nexturl field points to a page that will be sent in reply to the reader submitting the form. A simple thank you page with links back to other pages in the Webspace should do.

The gateway script uses the to, from, name, and sub fields to fill in the e-mail header information. The body and any other fields, nicely parsed and formatted, constitute the body of the e-mail message sent to the address value of the to field. For more information on Doug's WWW Mail Gateway, see:

```
http://www-bprc.mps.ohio-state.edu/mailto/mailto_info.html
```

CONVERTING AN EXISTING DOCUMENT TO HTML

In contrast to creating a home page, converting an existing document to hypertext is best approached from the bottom up. Suppose you have a user's guide for some aspect of your business. It could even be a guide to using the Internet. Let's assume that the document exists in the normal format of a word processing program such as Microsoft Word.

Working from the bottom up, you'll create a series of versions of the guide, each a refinement of the previous one. When the conversion is complete, you'll have a full hypertext version consisting of linked files, a single formatted version suitable for printing, a text-only version for readers with nongraphical browsers, and the original version in a format suitable for downloading. On top of all this, you'll create a home page for the guide that describes the work and has links to the various versions and to related works, as well as authorship and status information for the guide.

The first step is to create an ASCII text version of the guide. The file needs a bit of preparation before it's saved, however. Start with a copy of the MS Word file and substitute character entities for the markup characters, that is, globally change:

```
& to &amp;
 < to &lt;
 > to &gt;
```

and replace any "curly" quotes (', " ") with the straight ASCII versions (', " "). Any special characters from the ISO Latin-1 character set should also be replaced with their character entities at this point.

> **Note:** Many HTML editors will do all this prep work for you. If you have such an editor, just save a copy as a text file and let your HTML editor do the work.

Next, delete any unnecessary horizontal tabs like those used for paragraph indentation. You can decide later what to do with other tab marks; whether to use preformatted text, HTML tab stops, or table markup to re-create the original structure. Remove any headers and footers from the guide, since you have no control over how many lines a browser will display per page or screen and page numbering is not important in hypertext works.

Create a new directory for the project—let's call it guide. It can be a subdirectory of a Webspace or a sibling, whatever is appropriate to the relation of this work to your other hypertext works. Save a copy of the file in either "Text only" or "Text with line breaks" format. Put it in the guide directory and give it a file name with the extension, ".txt"8585. This is the file you will make available to readers with linemode browsers.

Go back to the original guide in your word processor's normal format. You can create the downloadable version from this file by stuffing and encoding it. Stuffing compacts the file by removing excess space; encoding creates a seven-bit portable version of the file, allowing it to be moved and stored as a text file on any kind of operating system.

From the original document capture any illustrations and figures in the text. Convert these to GIF format and save them in a subdirectory of the guide called images. Use a file-naming convention that preserves the image's location—for example, GUIDE03-F04.GIF—for the fourth figure in Chapter 3 of the guide. The leading zeros in the file name will insure proper sorting in a directory listing if you have more than nine items.

Edit the text-only version and make notations in the text where the illustrations and figures were and resave this file. Now, also save a copy of the file with the extension, ".html".

At the beginning of this new file create an HTML head section with the main title enclosed in title tags, followed by the starting tag for the body section, followed by the main title again as a level 1 heading. Place the matching end tags at the end of the file. It should look something like this:

```
<HTML>
<!-- guide.html, a hypertext guide to the Internet -->
<!-- Converted from MS Word file: INT_GUIDE          -->
<!-- J. Kepler, October 29, 1609.                    -->
<HEAD>
<TITLE>Internet Guide</TITLE>
</HEAD>
<BODY>
<H1>Internet Guide</H1>


{ rest of the file }


</BODY>
</HTML>
```

Next, starting from the beginning of the file, work your way through, placing line breaks (<BR>) and paragraph (<P></P>) tags where needed and enclosing headings in heading tags. Work with a printed copy of the original as a guide, but don't try to match specific font sizes with different heading levels. Use headings logically—level 2 for the major divisions of the guide, level 3 for the next level, and so on. As you go through the file, enclose any styled text with appropriate tags—<EM></EM> for text that should be emphasized, <STRONG></STRONG> for strongly emphasized text, <Q></Q> and <CITE></CITE> for quoted text and titles, and so forth. Try to avoid using the style tags <B></B>, <U></U>, and <I></I> unless that style is explicitly referred to within the text.

Look for places in the text where HTML lists or tables can be used to structure information. Likewise, footnotes and sidenotes should be identified and marked up with <FN></FN> and <NOTE></NOTE> tags. When you've completed this pass, the first draft of the HTML version of the guide is finished. Save this file. Your directory should now look something like Figure 4.7.

It's time to load your work into a browser and see what it looks like. Print it out and show it around. The next step is to go through the file adding internal anchors and links and inserting image and figure tags for the removed illustrations and figures. Make the text of each of the major headings a named anchor

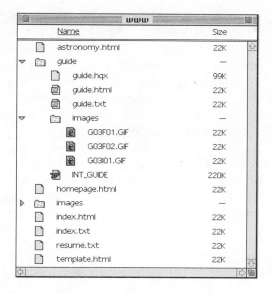

Figure 4.7: Directory listing with guide files

with the ID attribute. Use the heading's index from the table of contents as the name, for example:

```
<H3 ID="G32">3.2 Gopher</H3>
```

In the table of contents, create a link to each of these headings:

```
<LI><A HREF="#G32">3.2 Gopher</A>
```

If there are references to other documents on your network or references to re-sources on the Internet, create links to them as well. If you're not sure about the URL, make a guess. An incorrect URL will not crash the system; you can repair these bad links when you have the correct information.

When you are finished with this process you'll have the long hypertext ver-sion of the guide. This version will be more suitable for printing than your final version, but will still be fine for online browsing (although it may take some time for the entire file to load over a slow line). Take some time to clean up and test this version, using different browsers if possible. If the original guide had a glossary, an index, or a quick reference section, now is the time to decide how to implement these features.

When the long version is fairly stable, decide how to break it up into separate files. Having a hypertext work in a series of linked files has several advantages.

The individual files are faster to load and the reader can have more than one section of the work displayed at the same time. Ideally, no single part of the guide should be more than a dozen screens' worth of information. The exception to this is very long list structures, which should go into separate files for easier maintenance. The table of contents will go into the guide's home page. If a section of the guide is long and has many subsections, consider creating a mini-home page for that section with its own, linked mini-table of contents.

Each file will have to begin and end with the HTML tags defining the head and body of the page. Copy the title of the work as a whole and make it a level 1 heading as the very first element of the page body of each file so your readers know what they're reading. Put a horizontal rule under the level 1 heading and you have a page header. Here is what the beginning of the Chapter 3 page might look like:

```
<HTML>
<!-- guide-3.html, Chapter 3 of Internet Guide      -->
<!-- Converted from MS Word file: INT_GUIDE          -->
<!-- J. Kepler, Nov. 4, 1609.                        -->
<HEAD>
<TITLE>Internet Guide, Chap. 3</TITLE>
</HEAD>
<BODY>
<H1>Internet Guide</H1>
<HR>
<H2 ID="G30">Chapter 3 - Clients</H2>
A nice introductory paragraph should go here.
<H3>Contents</H3>
<OL>
<LI><A HREF="#G31">ftp</A>
<LI><A HREF="#G32">Gopher</A>
<LI><A HREF="#G33">...</A>
</OL>
<H3 ID="G31">3.1 ftp</H3>
```

Any links to anchors that are now in different files must be updated to include the file name of the destination. Links in other files to anchors in this file will also have to be updated. The home page for the entire guide will contain the table of contents, the introduction, the guide's authorship information (make your name a link to your personal home page), and links to related works.

A nice touch is to add a set of navigation buttons to the bottom of each page in the guide. This next bit of HTML, at the end of the file for Chapter 3, creates a set of four text buttons that link to other files of the guide. The last link, [CONTENTS], goes to an anchor named ToC on the guide's home page, the file GuideHome.html. You can also use small icons for these buttons. Following the buttons is a link back to the authorship information on the guide's home page.

```
<HR>
<A HREF="guidehome.html">[TOP]</A>
<A HREF="guide-2.html">[PREVIOUS]</A>
<A HREF="guide-4.html">[NEXT]</A>
<A HREF="guidehome.html#ToC">[CONTENTS]</A>
<ADDRESS>
<A HREF="guidehome.html#author">JK</A> -- Nov. 4, 1609
</ADDRESS>
</BODY>
</HTML>
```

Figure 4.8 shows what the Chapter 3 title page (minus a lot of the middle) might look like.

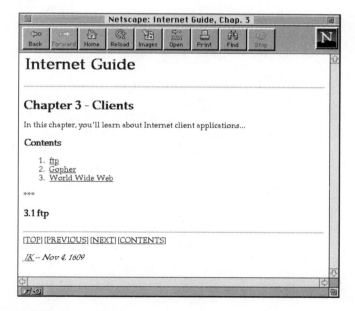

Figure 4.8: Title page for a chapter

Advanced Design

PAGE BACKGROUNDS

STYLE SHEETS

MORE ON IMAGES

IMAGEMAPS

MULTIMEDIA

I n this chapter we'll take up some of the techniques that make Web pages interesting. That's not to say that a page can't be interesting just for its content. But, with the possible exception of the Declaration of Independence, even the best material benefits from a nice, well thought-out design.

The first section of this chapter covers page backgrounds: how to set page and text colors and how to use an image to pattern the page. The second section covers style sheets and how to set colors and typographic styles for individual HTML elements. The third section provides more instruction on the use of figures and images including clickable imagemaps, and, finally, a section on multimedia—putting sound and video links on your page.

Page backgrounds

There are six attributes that can be used in the <BODY> tag to control the general look of a page. Two of the attributes, BACKGROUND and BGCOLOR control the look and color of the "paper" upon which the content is "printed." The other four attributes, TEXT, LINK, VLINK, and ALINK control the color of the various text states. What are these states? Well, the value of the TEXT attribute specifies the color of ordinary text which, by default, is almost always black. The value of the LINK attribute specifies the color of links, usually blue. VLINK is for the color of visited links—purple in Netscape—and ALINK is the color of active links, that is, the color seen while the mouse button is held down.

The BACKGROUND attribute's value is the URL of an image file, usually a small one in GIF format. For example,

```
<BODY BACKGROUND="images/bkground.gif">
```

When the page is loaded, the image is downloaded to the reader's disk just like any ordinary inline image. However, the browser repeats the image across and down the page forming a background pattern as in Figure 5.1.

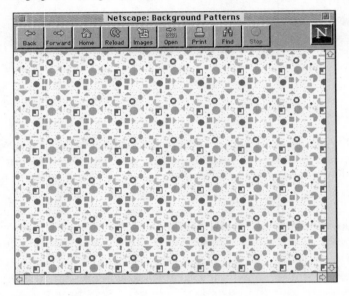

Figure 5.1: Background pattern

Background patterns can be very attractive, providing effects ranging from watermarks to fields of stars, and they're very easy to install. On a Macintosh, you can copy a pattern out of the Desktop Patterns control panel, paste it into a graphics application or utility and save it in GIF format. In Windows, you can open a bitmap file (the filename ends in ".bmp") in a graphic application or utility and similarly save it in GIF format. Just for fun, experiment with background images that are 1 pixel high.

There are a couple of things to be aware of when using a GIF as a background pattern. First, keep it small. The smaller it is, the faster your page will load. Second, use as few colors as possible. Some operating systems allow only a limited number of colors to be used in a page and there are many readers browsing the Web on 16-color and even grayscale machines. If the total number of colors used on a page exceeds the capacity of the reader's display device, the extra colors will be changed to colors in the existing set and the results can look quite ugly. So, be sure to check out your backgrounds at different color depths. Make sure your page is readable on those 16-color Windows systems and grayscale laptops. Color mapping across systems is problematic at best. If you have photographs on your page and you want them to look their best, avoid using background patterns.

The BGCOLOR attribute and the four text color attributes take rgb values. An rgb value is a triplet of red, green, and blue values, a universal method of specifying colors since any color in the visual spectrum can be expressed as a combination of these colors. In HTML, we specify a color like so:

`#rrggbb`

using two characters each for the red, the green, and the blue values, preceded by the pound sign.

Each red, green, and blue value is a hexadecimal number between 0 and 255. Hexadecimal. Yikes! Okay, I know, your eyes glazed over in that Introduction to Computers class when they talked about hexadecimal or base 16 arithmetic. Don't panic; in this context, it's not that difficult. For example, each of the two "r" characters representing the red value is a symbol standing for a number from 0 to 15. The first "r" is the number of "16s" and the second "r" is the number of "1s." Thus, hexadecimal 42 is four 16s (64) and two 1s, or decimal 66. The symbols used are the ordinary digits 0 through 9 for the numbers zero to nine and the letters "A" to "F" for the numbers 10 to 15.

The color black is the rgb value #000000, and full white is #FFFFFF. Any value that has identical rr, gg, and bb parts is a shade of gray. A body tag specifying a blue background is written:

`<BODY BGCOLOR="#0000FF">`

Mixing colors on a computer is an additive process—larger values mean more light is going into the final color. That's why #7F7FFF is light blue and not mud. Unfortunately this is a black-and-white book, so I can only give you the names of the colors corresponding to the values in the following table of common rgb values.

	Dark	Medium	Bright
Red	#400000	#7F0000	#FF0000
Yellow	#404000	#7F7F00	#FFFF00

	Dark	Medium	Bright
Green	#004000	#007F00	#00FF00
Cyan	#004040	#007F7F	#00FFFF
Blue	#000040	#00007F	#0000FF
Magenta	#400040	#7F007F	#FF00FF

Here is a body tag specifying a light yellow page background with dark green text. Linked text is rendered in bright pink that changes to a medium gray to indicate that the link has been recently taken:

```
<BODY BGCOLOR="#FFFF7F" TEXT="#004000" LINK="#FF00A0" VLINK="#A0A0A0">
```

What do you think would happen if the values of the BGCOLOR and VLINK attributes were the same? For example,

```
<BODY BGCOLOR="#C0C0C0" VLINK="#C0C0C0">
```

As with page backgrounds, be sure you check out how your page colors look on a grayscale laptop or a 16-color system.

For changing the color and size of individual text elements within the page body, there is a Netscape extension, the <FONT></FONT> tags. The font element should be used like other inline style elements, such as emphasis, inside of enclosing HTML structural elements. It has two attributes: SIZE and COLOR. The value of SIZE is a signed number from −3 to +3 indicating how much smaller or larger, relative to the current font size, to set the font size(s) of the enclosed content. The COLOR attribute takes an #rgb value as described above. For example, the following bit of HTML will be rendered in red type, moderately larger than corresponding elements on the rest of the page.

```
<P><FONT SIZE=+2 COLOR="#FF0000">!! Hot Sites !!</FONT></P>
```

When viewed in Netscape (on a color display), the text should be red and a couple of point sizes larger than normal paragraph text. The color applies only to normal text. It won't change the color of linked text.

STYLE SHEETS

Don't pay any attention to the information in this section. If you're just starting to mark up information in HTML you will need more practice and experience to fully understand and appreciate the benefits of an abstract approach to document presentation—how productive you can be once free of the design restraints imposed by specific media types and display devices. The essential idea behind HTML is to describe to any computer the content of your document instead of instructing a particular computer, step by step, how to build a document with the desired content. The Web author is encouraged to surrender control of his documents' layout and typography and trust the readers' browsers to do the right thing. However, this is the real world, and I don't blame you for wanting to have more control over your work. You fought hard for that control, so here, in this section on style sheets, are the HTML elements for more precise control over typographic styles and layout elements.

One more reason for skipping this section: At the time of this writing, there are only a couple of browsers in beta testing that support style sheets. The following material is based only on a proposed draft specification (fifth revision) for "cascading style sheets." It's available at <http://www.w3.org/pub/WWW/Style/css/draft.html>. It's an overview only—just to give an idea of how style sheets work. Before you start to author Web pages using style sheets, you'll have to read the release notes for your browser for the set of features available and the exact syntax required. To me, the most useful feature of style sheets is the control of colors on a page.

Cascading Style Sheets provide precise typographic control over specific HTML elements in a Web page. They are called cascading because, at each level, the styles applicable to any text content is inherited from the levels above. At the highest level, style declarations can be in an external file that is referenced from the current document. A <LINK> tag in the document's head does the trick:

```
<HEAD>
<TITLE>Page of Style</TITLE>
<LINK REL="stylesheet" HREF="./styles/common.css">
</HEAD>
```

Actually, there's a level above this. If a browser recognizes style sheets, it should also allow the override of author's styles with the reader's preferences. A document can have multiple links to style sheets. However, it's more usual to have just a single reference to a common style sheet file followed by specific style declarations, for example:

```
<HEAD>
<TITLE>Page of Style</TITLE>
<LINK REL="stylesheet" HREF="./styles/common.css">
<STYLE NOTATION="CSS">
   H1 {font-family: sans-serif}
```

```
      H2 {color: blue}
</STYLE>
</HEAD>
```

The "sans-serif" style instructs the browser to choose a simple font, such as helvetica, for all level 1 heading text. All other text in the document will use the normal font unless specifically overridden by later style declarations, or styles inherited from higher levels.

Additional styles per elements are separated by commas:

```
<STYLE NOTATION="CSS">
   H1 {font-family: sans-serif}
   H2 {color: blue, align: center, font-style: italic}
</STYLE>
```

The HTML element name beginning a style declaration is called the selector. To apply a style to an entire document, use an asterisk (*) as the selector.

```
<STYLE NOTATION="CSS">
   * {font-size: large}
</STYLE>
```

A number of selectors can be listed together, separated by commas. The following declaration will cause all headings to be rendered using small caps.

```
<STYLE NOTATION="CSS">
   H1, H2, H3, H4, H5, H6 {font-style: small-caps}
</STYLE>
```

One selector can be used to constrain another. For example, looking at a previous declaration:

```
H2 {color: blue, align: center, font-style: italic}
```

we see that emphasized text, which is usually rendered in italic, would be indistinguishable inside a level 2 heading. What is needed is a way to declare a style for emphasized text only when inside a level 2 heading. We do that by putting the first selector in parentheses, as in this declaration:

```
(H2) EM {color: cyan, font-family: normal}
```

which changes the color of heading level 2, emphasized text to cyan and resets the font style (for readers without color displays) back to normal.

All paragraphs are not the same. The real power of style sheets comes with the use of classes. The CLASS attribute can be added to any HTML block element to subclass the nature of that element. For example, suppose we have one or more paragraphs like the following in the body of our page:

```
<P CLASS="legal">
Before clicking on the "accept" button, carefully read the
terms and conditions of this agreement.  By clicking on the
"accept" button, you are consenting to be bound by and are
becoming a party to this agreement.  If you do not agree to all
of the terms of this agreement, click the "do not accept"
button.</P>
```

We can apply styles to all "legal" paragraphs in our document with the following style declaration:

```
<STYLE NOTATION="CSS">
   P.legal {font-family: serif,
            font-style: small-caps,
            align: justify}
</STYLE>
```

Class names can be used as selectors in the same manner as HTML element names. In the following HTML, all of the content between the starting and ending <DIV> tags will rendered in a green and unusual (browser dependent) font, aligned to the right margin, except for level 3 headings and unordered lists, which will be aligned right:

```
<HEAD>
<TITLE>...</TITLE>
<STYLE NOTATION="CSS">
   farout  {font-family: fantasy,
            color: green,
            align: right}
   H3, UL {align: left}
</STYLE>
</HEAD>
<BODY>
  .
  .
<DIV CLASS="farout">
<!-- GOING WILD FOR THIS SECTION OF THE PAGE -->
  .
  .
</DIV>
</BODY>
```

Style sheet specifications can get quite intricate and the more intricate the specification the more you will have to know about the capabilities of your readers' browsers. At the time of this writing, style sheets are still too new to predict which of several formats will become the market leader or the official standard. Cascading style sheets are a good bet right now because they provide generality and extensibility of features. Still, it's not at all clear that there will be only one way to add styles to a Web page. Style sheets are most useful, therefore, for publishing on internal Webs; as within a corporation that has standardized on a single browser.

More on images

An inline image behaves on a Web page as if it were a large character of text. It is inserted into the content at a specific point in the text. I mention this again because it is the key to understanding how to use images on a Web page. First of all, it means anywhere you can put a character of text, you can put an inline image. Secondly, inline images are bound to adjacent characters or other inline images the same way as letters are bound into words. This means that:

```
<IMG SRC="...">
<IMG SRC="...">
<IMG SRC="...">
```

is not the same as:

```
<IMG SRC="..."><IMG SRC="..."><IMG SRC="...">
```

In the former case, the carriage returns ending each line in your HTML source file appear as spaces between the images. In the latter, there are no spaces whatsoever between the images.

A large image, especially one that's wider than it is high, should be placed by itself, either by enclosing it in line break tags, or better yet, an HTML element that can take the ALIGN attribute, such as a division, heading, or paragraph. The following HTML, for example, centers an image over a "caption":

```
<H3 ALIGN=center><IMG SRC="images/300-8.gif"><BR>
Cover of the First Edition</H3>
```

Figure 5.2 shows how this would be rendered.

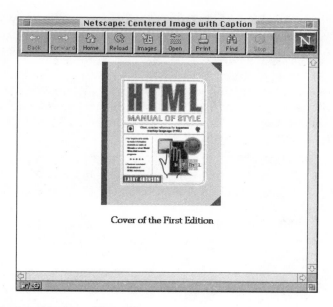

Figure 5.2: Centered image with caption

WRAP-AROUND TEXT

For images that are taller than they are wide, we often want text to flow around the image, either on the left or the right side. There are two approaches in HTML for doing this. The first method was introduced as an extension in Netscape to the HTML2 image element and has been widely accepted by other browser manufacturers. The second and newer approach is the HTML3 figure element.

Netscape extended the ALIGN attribute so that it recognized the values "right" and "left." ALIGN=left means that the image is rendered to the left side of the text, and ALIGN=right means that the image is rendered to the right of the text. This is distinctly different from the values of "top," "middle," and "bottom," which specify how the image should be aligned with the baseline of the text. When the ALIGN attribute has a value of "right" or "left," the image is no longer inserted at a specific point like a character that word-wraps with the rest of the text. The image now behaves as a container. There is no ending image tag, </IMG>, to signal the end of the container; rather, any HTML element with the CLEAR attribute stops the text from flowing around the image. Since the image is not tied to a specific point, you should be careful in placing it inside other HTML elements; headings, for example.

Figure 5.3, generated by the following HTML, shows a right-aligned image.

```
<HR>
<IMG SRC="images/300-8s.gif" ALIGN=right ALT="cover">
<H3><CITE>HTML Manual of Style</CITE>,</H3>
Published by Ziff-Davis Press, was one of the very first books
on World Wide Web publishing. It's now in its fifth printing
and available in several foreign translations.<BR CLEAR=right>
<HR>
```

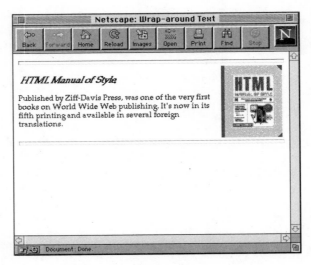

Figure 5.3: An image with wrap-around text

The line break tag specified with CLEAR=right in the above example instructs the browser to space down the page, if necessary, until the current right margin is clear before placing the next HTML element, in this case, a horizontal rule. There are no restrictions on what other HTML elements can be inside the content that flows around an image. You can have headings, lists, tables, even other images. For example, Figure 5.4 shows what happens when the same image is used with both left and right alignment. It's generated by the following HTML.

```
<HTML>
<HEAD>
<TITLE>Image Alignment</TITLE>
</HEAD>
```

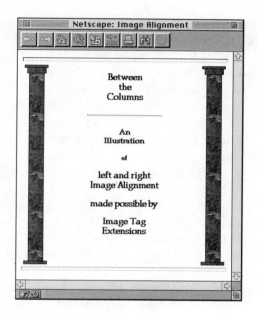

Figure 5.4: Left and right image alignment

```
<BODY>
<HR SIZE=6 CLEAR>
<IMG ALIGN=left SRC="images/COLUMN.GIF">
<IMG ALIGN=right SRC="images/COLUMN.GIF">
<PRE></PRE>  <!-- force a little spacing at the top -->
<H3 ALIGN=center>Between<BR>the<BR>Columns</H3>
<HR ALIGN=center WIDTH=50%>
<H4 ALIGN=center>An<BR>Illustration</H4>
<H5 ALIGN=center>of</H5>
<H3 ALIGN=center>left and right<BR>Image Alignment</H3>
<H3 ALIGN=center>made possible</H3>
<H5 ALIGN=center>by</H5>
<H3 ALIGN=center>Extensions</H3>
<H5 ALIGN=center>to the</H5>
<H3 ALIGN=center>Image Tag</H3>
<HR SIZE=6 CLEAR>
</BODY>
</HTML>
```

For a little more control, Netscape recognizes the additional attributes, HSPACE and VSPACE. These attributes take a numeric value specifying the number of pixels of padding that should be placed between the image and the text that flows around it. HSPACE is the space on the right or left of the image, VSPACE is the amount of space above and below the image. Generally speaking, the larger the image, the more HSPACE and VSPACE you'll want. Typical values are from five to 15 pixels. This is different from the BORDER attribute which applies only when the image is inside an anchor tag. When it's obvious that an image is a button that the reader may click on, you can suppress the blue border indicating that the image is a link by adding BORDER=0 102to the image tag.

There is another set of Netscape image extensions: the attributes HEIGHT and WIDTH, which also take values in pixels, but their function in the image tag is performance-related. If you specify the HEIGHT and WIDTH attributes, the Netscape browser will pre-allocate a rectangle of that shape in the appropriate place on the page. This allows the browser to continue formatting the page while the image is being downloaded; speeding up the process for the reader.

The HEIGHT and WIDTH attributes should be given values that are the exact vertical and horizontal size of the image. If you provide values that are different than the actual size of the image, Netscape will attempt to scale the image to that size, however, it does not use a very sophisticated algorithm. So, if you want to change the size of an image, it's better to do so in Photoshop or some other graphic application. There's one exception to this rule, however: Netscape has one more image tag attribute to improve loading performance, LOWSRC. This attribute, which takes an URL in the same manner as the SRC attribute, loads an image before the image specified by the URL of the SRC attribute. Suppose you have an image that's 300 × 400 pixels. Use a graphics utility to create a smaller copy that has the same proportions, say 30 × 40 pixels. For simplicity, we will call the two image files large.gif and small.gif. Write the image tag as follows:

```
<IMG LOWSRC="small.gif" SRC="large.gif" WIDTH=300 HEIGHT=400>
```

When Netscape processes this tag, it will download small.gif first and scale it up to 300 × 400 pixels. Since the file is small, it will load very fast. It will appear as a low resolution image, because when you originally scaled it from 300 × 400 pixels down to 30 × 40, you threw out 99 percent of the data. Netscape can continue to load and format the rest of the page's content. Then, when the download of large.gif is complete, it will replace small.gif with large.gif in the same frame.

This next example shows how to combine many of the image attributes discussed above. It's the two by three table of images and text shown in Figure 5.5. Here's the HTML:

```
<HTML>
<HEAD>
<TITLE>Image Table</TITLE>
</HEAD>
<BODY>
<TABLE CELLSPACING=10>
<TR>
<TD><IMG SRC="images/A.gif" ALIGN=left HSPACE=5 HEIGHT=72 WIDTH=60>
    Athena<BR>Anubis<BR>Ariel<BR>Aphrodite</TD>
<TD><IMG SRC="images/B.gif" ALIGN=left HSPACE=5 HEIGHT=72 WIDTH=60>
    Baal<BR>Bragi<BR>Bubastis<BR>Bigfoot</TD>
<TD><IMG SRC="images/C.gif" ALIGN=left HSPACE=5 HEIGHT=72 WIDTH=60>
    Cassiopeia<BR>Cronus<BR>Cupid<BR>Ceres</TD>
</TR>
<TR>
<TD><IMG SRC="images/D.gif" ALIGN=left HSPACE=5 HEIGHT=72 WIDTH=60>
    Diana<BR>Dionysus<BR>Demeter<BR>Doctor Who</TD>
<TD><IMG SRC="images/E.gif" ALIGN=left HSPACE=5 HEIGHT=72 WIDTH=60>
    Ea<BR>Eros<BR>Elvis<BR>Electra</TD>
<TD><IMG SRC="images/F.gif" ALIGN=left HSPACE=5 HEIGHT=72 WIDTH=60>
    Fatima<BR>Flora<BR>Freya<BR>Frankenstein</TD>
</TR>
</TABLE>
</BODY>
</HTML>
```

FIGURES

Unlike Netscape's extensions to the image tag for wrap-around text, the figure element is a true container. It encompasses much of the same functionality as the Netscape extensions to the image tag, but does so with sub-elements, instead of additional attributes.

In the publishing world, figures are differentiated from illustrations in that the former have captions and the latter do not. To add a caption to a figure, the <CAPTION></CAPTION> sub-element is used. Another sub-element <CREDIT></CREDIT> can be used to provide source information. The syntax of the caption tag is the same as that of the table caption element, taking

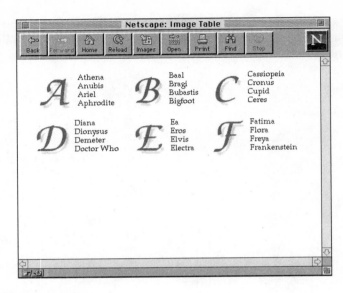

Figure 5.5: Images in a table

an ALIGN attribute with a value of either "top" or "bottom." The figure tag it-self can have the usual values of "left," "center," or "right" as the value of the ALIGN attribute. The default value is "center" which disables text flow. Values of "left" or "right" will force text to flow around the right or left side, respectively, of the figure. For example:

```
<FIG SRC="images/internet.gif" ALIGN=right>
<CAPTION ALIGN=bottom>Internet Growth</CAPTION>
This is the final frame of a movie made by researchers at the National
Center for Super computing Activities (NCSA) at the University of
Illinois to show the growth in Internet traffic over the NSFnet.
<CREDIT>Cox/NCSA</CREDIT>
</FIG>
```

Figure 5.6 shows how this would be displayed in an HTML3 browser.

Another figure sub-element is the <OVERLAY> tag. Like the image tag, the overlay tag is an empty tag, taking an SRC attribute to point to an image file. The purpose of the OVERLAY tag is to permit authors to specify a single base figure to be used on several pages with other image elements, specific to each page, layered on top of it. This can improve performance since the base figure will only be downloaded once and can be fetched from the reader's cache for

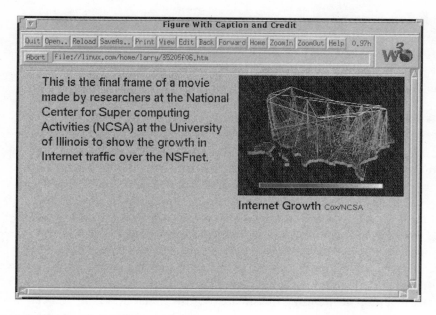

Figure 5.6: Figure with caption and credit

each subsequent page. To position the overlay on the base figure, use the X and Y attributes with values in pixels specifying the position of the top left corner of the overlay with respect to the top left corner of the base figure. For example, this bit of HTML:

```
<FIG SRC="images/basefig.gif" HEIGHT=200 WIDTH=400>
<OVERLAY SRC="images/ovly_01.gif" HEIGHT=50 WIDTH=50 X=350 Y=0>
</FIG>
```

will display a base figure, aligned in the center of the page (the default) with an overlaid, square image occupying the top right corner.

IMAGEMAPS

Imagemaps are an important extension to the concept of document linking. An imagemap is an ordinary image or figure upon which a set of subareas have been defined, each of which can link, when clicked in, to a different URL. There are currently three different methods of designating such subareas: the original HTML2 method, a set of Netscape extensions to the image tag, and an HTML3 extension to the anchor tag used in conjunction with the figure element. The

HTML2 method is referred to as server-side imagemaps, since it requires a special program residing on the server called imagemap. The other two methods are referred to as client-side imagemaps, since they do not require any processing on the server, and thus, unlike the HTML2 method, can be developed and tested locally.

SERVER-SIDE IMAGEMAPS

Server-side imagemaps are supported by most browsers that can display images, and will be discussed first. Implementing a server-side imagemap requires root access to the server, so you'll probably need the assistance of your Webmaster or systems administrator. Client-side imagemaps are much easier, however, they are newer and not yet as widely supported. You can expect support for both client-side methods to increase as they offer significant advantages over server-side processing of imagemaps.

The key to server-side imagemaps is the inclusion of the attribute ISMAP in the image tag (it does not take a value), and the enclosing of the image tag in an anchor tag that links to the imagemap program on the server passing a pointer to a map file defining the subareas of the image and their associated URLs. Unfortunately, the exact syntax of all the various pieces of this process differs slightly depending on the type of server software used. Here's an example using the syntax appropriate to NCSA's UNIX-based http server. It is also valid for Starnine's Macintosh-based Webstar server and many others:

```
<A HREF="http://www.yerserver.com/cgi-bin/imagemap/demo">
<IMG SRC="images/demo.gif" WIDTH=300 HEIGHT=200 ISMAP></A>
```

The special directory cgi-bin exists at the root of most Web servers. It's the repository of cgi (Common Gateway Interface) scripts. Imagemap is the name of one such script supplied with most server software. See the documentation at <http://hoohoo.ncsa.uiuc.edu/cgi/overview.html> for more information. Readers with some UNIX experience would interpret the above URL to reference a file named "demo" in a directory named "imagemap," but this is not the case. Web servers will interpret "demo" as extra path information that is passed to the imagemap program, in an environmental variable (PATH_INFO). The imagemap program treats this information as a symbolic name which it looks up in a special configuration file (imagemap.conf). This information allows it to find the actual path and file containing the information that maps subareas of the image to specific URLs. This file is called a map file. By convention, it has the same name as the image file but ends in ".map" instead of ".gif". It can be located in your webspace, so you have the ability to change the imagemap's subareas just as long as you don't change the name or location of the map file.

The map file is an ASCII text file with one line per image subarea specifying the shape of the subarea, the URL linked to that subarea, and the subarea's coordinates. In our example, it would be called demo.map, and a line in this file defining a 50×50 pixel subarea in the upper-right corner of our 300×200 image would look something like:

```
rect     http://www.someplace.com/somepage.html     249,0 299,49
```

"rect" says that the shape of the subarea is a rectangle and that the coordinates (x,y x,y) are the offset of the top-left and bottom-right corners, inclusive, from the top-left corner of the image. The URL should always be specified in its full format. Other entries can be "circle," with coordinates referring to the center and any point on the circumference, "poly," with n sets of coordinates specifying the vertices of a polygon with n sides, and "default," with no coordinates providing an URL to link to when the reader clicks outside of any defined subarea. Subareas can overlap, in which case the first entry matching the coordinates of the reader's mouse click will be used.

CLIENT-SIDE IMAGEMAPS

There is an elegant implementation of client-side imagemaps that's flexible and can be used in conjunction with server-side imagemaps for browsers that don't support these extensions. Either in place of, or in addition to the image tag's ISMAP attribute, you can code the USEMAP attribute, the value of which is an URL pointing to a map specification element. This element can be in the same file as the image tag with the USEMAP attribute, in a separate file by itself, or in a file with other map specifications. Here's an example of a "button-bar" with a three-button map in the same file as the image tag:

```
<IMG SRC="images/bbar.gif" WIDTH=150 HEIGHT=30 USEMAP="#bbar">

<MAP NAME="bbar">
<AREA SHAPE="rect" HREF="top.html" COORDS="0,0,49,29">
<AREA SHAPE="rect" HREF="prev.html" COORDS="50,0,99,29">
<AREA SHAPE="rect" HREF="next.html" COORDS="100,0,149,29">
</MAP>
```

The USEMAP attribute takes precedence over an ISMAP attribute. Thus, if a reader's browser does not support such client-side imagemaps, it will ignore the USEMAP attribute and the <MAP></MAP> and <AREA> tags and process the imagemap using the HTML2 server-side mechanism. Note the differences in syntax between server-side and client-side map specifications. The latter uses relative URL addressing and requires a comma between the top-left and bottom-right coordinates.

Like server-side imagemap processing, the first <AREA> specification that matches the coordinates of the reader's mouse click will be the one taken. To provide a default URL for reader clicks outside any defined subareas, you only have to provide a final <AREA> with coordinates encompassing the entire image area. If it is desired that such a default take no action; that no link be made, then NOHREF is used in place of HREF="url".

The HTML3 specification allows for a different method of implementing client-side imagemaps. Within the content contained in the HTML3 figure element, anchors can have the additional attribute, SHAPE, which takes a set of coordinate values. This was done to encourage authors to provide descriptive links in the text corresponding to the subareas defined in the figure for non-complying browsers. This works nicely for many simple application interface screens, especially when used with the <OVERLAY> sub-element. However, it can get awkward when the imagemap has many subareas; on a state map of counties, for example. Of course, one does not have to provide any content between the starting and ending anchor tags. For example, to implement the button bar in the example above using the figure element, you would code:

```
<FIG SRC="images/bbar.gif">
<A HREF="top.html" SHAPE="0,0,49,29"></A>
<A HREF="prev.html" SHAPE="50,0,99,29"></A>
<A HREF="next.html" SHAPE="100,0,149,29"></A>
</FIG>
```

An HTML2 browser will not recognize the figure tag and no image or anchor text will appear on the page.

MULTIMEDIA

Despite all the excitement generated by multimedia Web pages, there's really not much to learn about coding them in HTML. The process of creating multimedia objects, on the other hand, is very involved, platform specific, and beyond the scope of this book.

To include a multimedia object on your Web page, be it a sound bite, or a video clip, or whatever, just create a normal link to the binary file containing the object. It is up to the reader to configure his or her browser to recognize the object by the file name extension and associate it with a suitable helper application on her computer.

It is considered polite to inform your readers when a link is to some object other than a Web page, and to provide the size of the object so the reader can estimate how long it will take to download. For example, on the page containing information on the First Family in the White House's (the one on Washington DC, USA) Webspace, there is an image (an audio icon) that links to a sound file of the first feline's (Socks's) meow:

```
<A HREF="../audio/socks.au">
<IMG SRC="/White_House/images/audio_button.gif"
ALT="[AUDIO: Socks, the First Family's cat]"></A> (~36K)
```

Interactivity

CGI—Common Gateway Interface

Server-side includes

Client-pull and server-push

Persistent HTTP cookies

Applets—Java

Chapter
6

S o far, most of the material in this book has been directed towards publishing on the World Wide Web in the traditional sense of the word. Not in the traditional sense of the Web; it's not old enough yet to have a tradition. What I mean is in the traditional presentation model of publishing. A fixed amount of information is put on a "page" and presented to the reader. The Web, from this point of view, is the whole world's shared disk drive, with a graphic, hypertext-based file system. While this advance alone makes the Web the hottest thing since Pong, in the future the true value of the Web will be as an environment for distributed applications. In this environment, the reader, through his or her Web browser, will exist in a virtual space interacting with other intelligent objects.

We're not quite there yet. At this writing, most interactive Web applications use a server-side process called the Common Gateway Interface. However, several technologies are currently in beta testing that will, in response to a click on a link, download a small program to the reader's browser. This program will modify the current page in response to input from the reader. Such client-side programs are called "applets." In their present stage of development, applets are written by programmers in special computer languages. This chapter provides an overview of one such approach, Java, from Sun Microsystems. Before that, however, we'll review some of the current server-side technologies for adding dynamic content to a Web page.

CGI—COMMON GATEWAY INTERFACE

The Common Gateway Interface (CGI) is the Web's standard for client-server application interfacing. Most HTML documents are static, meaning that they exist in a constant state over some period of time, from hours to years. A CGI program, on the other hand, generates HTML in real time. Its output is a dynamically generated Web page. It's a way to present information to your readers that isn't exactly known until asked for.

CGI programs (or "scripts"—the terms are used interchangeably) perform many general Web functions. Imagemap, the CGI program that handles server-side imagemaps for many servers, is probably the most familiar. HTML forms typically require CGI scripts to do something with the information the readers enter. CGI scripts serve as the interface between a Web server and other computer applications, such as database managers and order processing systems. There's really no limit as to what can be hooked up to the Web. The only requirement is that a CGI program must do its work quickly. Otherwise, the reader will just be staring at their browser waiting for something to happen.

For most servers, CGI programs need to reside in a special directory, usually called cgi-bin, so that the Web server knows to execute the program rather than download it to the reader's browser. This directory is usually located at the root of the system, and can only be modified by your site's Webmaster. There are other ways to allow access to CGI scripts, but your Webmaster has to set these up for you, too. A program in the cgi-bin directory is meant to be executed by anyone. There's no built-in protection in this interface, so the Webmaster must have the final authority on the contents of that directory in order to keep the system secure.

A CGI program can be written in any language that allows it to be executed on the system hosting the Web server. Most are written in one of the following languages:

- ▶ C/C++
- ▶ FORTRAN
- ▶ PERL
- ▶ TCL
- ▶ UNIX shell
- ▶ Visual Basic
- ▶ AppleScript

In the simplest sense, information sent from the reader's browser goes to the CGI program as standard input, and whatever the program writes to standard output goes back to the reader. To understand it in more detail, it helps to understand a little more about Hypertext Transport Protocol (HTTP), the set of formal rules that servers and browsers follow when talking to each other. The conversation begins when the reader clicks on a link, or a form's submit button. It proceeds in four steps:

1 A connection is made to the server at the Internet address and port number specified in the URL.

2 The browser sends either a request to GET an object from the server, or a request to POST data to an object on the server.

3 The server sends back a response consisting of status code and usually, but not always, response data.

4 The browser closes the connection to the server.

The request data sent by the browser to the server includes a modified URL. The URL method (for example, http:) and the server:port address are stripped from the beginning of the URL and a query string preceded by a question mark (?) may be added to the end. When clicking on a (server-side) imagemap, for example, the request sent to the server will look like this:

```
GET /cgi-bin/imagemap/mapname?x,y HTTP/1.0
```

where "mapname" is the symbolic name (see Chapter 5) of the image's map file and (x,y) are the offset, in pixels, of the reader's click from the top-left corner of the image.

When the browser sends a request to the server using the POST method—the recommended method to use for forms—the information is sent as MIME data encoded in the standard URL format with spaces replaced by +, fields separated by ampersands (&), and special characters encoded in %xx hexadecimal notation. For a typical guestbook form, the actual request would look something like this:

```
POST /cgi-bin/guestbook.pl HTTP/1.0
Accept: text/plain
Accept: text/html
    .

    .
Accept: */*
Content-type: application/x-www-form-urlencoded
```

```
Content-length: 57
```

```
name=Larry+Aronson&addr=laronson@acm.org&loc=...
```

The script, guestbook.pl, would parse the data at the end of the request, append it to a file, or do something else with it and write a response to standard output. The server will send the output back to the reader along with a status code, such as 200 = success, or 404 = URL not found. To dynamically generate and return an HTML page, the output must begin with a MIME content declaration followed by an empty line followed by the HTML content. For example, the following UNIX shell script can be called by the CGI script processing our guestbook to generate the page shown in Figure 6.1:

```
#!/bin/sh
echo "Content-type: text/html"
echo
echo "<HEAD><TITLE>Guestbook Reply</TITLE></HEAD>"
echo "<BODY>"
echo "<H2 ALIGN=center>Thank You</H2>"
echo "<H3 ALIGN=center>for signing our GuestBook.</H3>"
echo "<HR>"
echo "Return to our <A HREF=\"/homepage.html\">homepage</A>"
echo "<P>"
echo "Go to the <A HREF=\"/visitors.html\">visitor's page</A>"
echo "</BODY>"
```

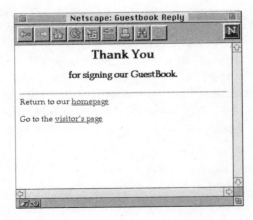

Figure 6.1: Dynamically generated page

A CGI script can direct the browser to load a new page by just supplying the URL:

```
#!/bin/sh
echo "Location: http://www.yerserver.com/replypage.html"
echo
```

There is, of course, much more to CGI scripting. The CGI script has access to a set of environmental variables set by the server. These variables contain additional information of use to a script, such as the client's Internet address and the browser software making the request. You'll have to check your server's documentation for the complete set of environment variables available for your scripts. To include all the varieties for the various different server/operating system combinations would turn this into a fat computer book. There's a good online primer for learning more about CGI at: <http://hoohoo.ncsa.uiuc.edu/>.

SERVER-SIDE INCLUDES

Server-side includes are a method of having the server insert content into a Web page as it is downloading it to the reader. Such content can be marked up text from another HTML file—a common banner for the top of every page in a Webspace, for example. The included content can also come from environmental variables set by the server and from information in the HTTP request block sent by the browser requesting the page. The content can even be generated by a CGI script.

Not all Web servers support server-side includes—NCSA's and Netscape's servers can; CERN's cannot—and many sites turn the feature off or restrict its use. There are two reasons for doing this. First, parsing every document requested, looking for includes, and patching the content eats up a lot of processing time. Second, there are security concerns when anyone can execute commands and launch programs just by downloading a page from your server.

Those Web sites that do support server-side includes usually restrict the parsing of documents to files with the special extension ".shtml" instead of ".html" or ".htm". Very few public sites support the execution of commands or scripts from server-side include declarations. Check first with your systems administrator to see what features are available for you to use.

The mechanism for specifying server-side includes uses a special form of the SGML/HTML comment:

```
<!--#command arg1="value1" arg2="value2" -->
```

The arguments are written in the same keyword=value format as tag attributes. There cannot be any spaces separating the opening left angle bracket (<), the exclamation point (!), dashes (--), and pound sign (#). There also cannot be any extra text. It may look like a comment, but it isn't.

The include command is one of the following:

- ▶ **include**   Inserts content from another file at the given point in the document

- ▶ **echo**   Inserts the value of a CGI environmental value at the given point in the document

- ▶ **exec**   Executes a shell command or a CGI script and inserts the output at the given point in the document

- ▶ **fsize**   Inserts the size, in bytes, of a specified file; useful for annotating links to files that vary in size, such as mail archives

- ▶ **flastmod**   Inserts the last modified timestamp of a specified file; useful for annotating links to files that are updated irregularly

Include, fsize, and flastmod take one of two arguments specifying the file to be included or reported on. That file must be on the same web server as the page containing the include. This include, for example:

```
<!--#include virtual="~www_admin/includes/logo_head.html"-->
```

uses the virtual argument and specifies the file by giving its path relative to the Web server. The tilde (~) is a UNIX shortcut meaning "the home directory of userid:". Here it is the file *logo_head.html* in a subdirectory, *includes*, of the home directory of the userid, *www_admin*. The other way of specifying the include file is with the "file" argument identifying a file relative to the parsed document's location. For example:

```
<!--#include file="my_buttons.html"-->
```

references an HTML file in the same directory as the HTML file containing the include. When using the file argument, the referenced file must be in the same directory or in a subdirectory of the file containing the include. It cannot be in a higher level directory.

The "echo" include command has one argument, var, which has as its value the name of an environmental variable. Just below is an example using three echo includes. The set of available environmental variables differs from one site to another as well as among different browsers, so I won't list them all. Check with your Webmaster to see which, if any, are available at your site.

```
<P>Welcome <!--#echo var="REMOTE_USER"--> to our Home Page.<BR>
It is now: <!--#echo var="DATE_LOCAL"-->.<BR>
This page was last modified on: <!--#echo var="LAST_MODIFIED"--
>.</P>
```

The exec include command has the single argument, *cmd,* with a value of a shell language command or the name of a CGI script. As mentioned above, Web sites rarely enable this feature as it eats up too much processing time and carries with it serious security concerns. Given the choice, most Web site administrators would rather have readers link directly to a script that dynamically generates an entire page rather than have the system include dynamically generated content into static, parsed pages.

CLIENT-PULL AND SERVER-PUSH

Browsers are generally driven by user input. The reader clicks on a link and a Web page is downloaded to the browser for viewing. Netscape, in release 1.1 of their Navigator browser, introduced a concept called dynamic documents. They come in two forms: client-pull and server-push. When a reader links to a client-pull page it is downloaded and displayed as usual. If, after a specified period of time, the reader has not clicked a link or otherwise exited the page, a second page is automatically sent to replace the first. A server-push document is a page, some part of which is continually refreshed by a server-side CGI script. Server-push provides a means for enhancing pages with inline animations. Let's look at client-pull pages first.

CLIENT-PULL

In this form of dynamic document, a special tag in the head section of the document tells the client what to do after some specified time has elapsed. In the simplest case the page is just automatically reloaded on a regular basis. For example, save the following HTML in a file:

```
<HTML>
<HEAD>
<META HTTP-EQUIV="Refresh" CONTENT=5>
<TITLE>Page One</TITLE>
</HEAD>
<BODY>
<H1>This is PAGE ONE!</H1>
```

```
Put some stuff here, maybe an image.
</BODY>
</HTML>
```

and load it into Netscape or some other browser that supports client-pull (not all browsers do.) You will notice that the page reloads itself once every five seconds.

It's the META tag in the head section that is, in effect, pulling a new copy of the page from the server every five seconds. The META tag simulates an HTTP response five seconds after being read by your browser. To the server, this response contains the request to reload the current page, just as if you had clicked the reload button. Each time the page is reloaded, the refresh directive is also reloaded. Thus, the page reloads itself every five seconds, until the reader intervenes and exits the page by clicking a link, or the home button, or by closing the page's window.

A client-pull page need not necessarily be a static page. If a process on the server periodically updates the HTML file with time dependent content, then the page is dynamically updating itself.

The META tag can also be used to cause another page to replace the current page in so many seconds.

```
<META HTTP-EQUIV="Refresh" CONTENT="60;
URL=http://yersite.com/page_2.html">
```

Note that a fully qualified URL is used and that a semicolon separates the two parts of the CONTENT attribute. This page can also be a client-pull page, making it possible to present a sequence of pages to the completely passive reader. Since not all browsers support the META tag, it's a good idea to explain near the top of the page that it might go away in so many seconds or minutes (or that it might not), and encourage your reader to click on one of the links provided.

SERVER-PUSH

In server-push, a server-side CGI script sends down a chunk of data which the browser displays normally. The HTTP connection, however, is kept open, allowing the server to send additional data whenever it wants to. The connection is held open for an indefinite period of time with each block of data replacing the previous until either the server decides enough is enough, or the reader interrupts the process or exits the page.

In a typical application, a block of data is a new HTML page, differing from the previous page in that some small part—a table of data read from a database (enclosed in <PRE></PRE> tags), for instance. This is like client-pull except that the control and timing are handled on the server side. It's also more efficient since the connection is opened and closed only once. However, it can use up considerable CPU resources on a server.

A Netscape extension provides another use—animation. The data sent by the server script can be a series of GIF images that are the frames of an animation. In the HTML for the page displaying this animation an ordinary image tag is used; *ordinary* except that the URL of the SRC attribute is a CGI script instead of a GIF file. For example, this image tag points to a CGI script on Netscape Communication's Web server:

```
<IMG WIDTH=64 HEIGHT=64 SRC="http://www.netscape.com/cgi-bin/doit.cgi">
```

doit.cgi is a small C program written by Rob McCool. You can get the source from: http://home.netscape.com/assist/net_sites/mozilla/doit.c. Like a CGI script it begins with a MIME content type/subtype declaration. However, instead of the usual "text/html" it writes the special declaration:

```
Content-type: multipart/x-mixed-replace;boundary=ThisRandomString
```

Typically, an HTTP response is only a single piece of data. However, the MIME standard has a facility for sending many pieces of data in a single response. So, the MIME type is "multipart" and the subtype says the data is of an experimental, mixed type that replaces previous data sent. The boundary argument provides a string that separates the data blocks. Each data block has its own MIME content type/subtype declaration—"text/html" for an HTML page, and "image/gif" for images, as in this case.

What doit.cgi does is run a timed loop that, during each iteration writes out the boundary string, a MIME declaration, and GIF data. Each iteration creates one frame of the animation. The output of doit.cgi looks like this:

```
Content-type: multipart/x-mixed-replace;boundary=---ThisRandomString
--ThisRandomString
Content-type: image/gif
{ GIF Data for the first frame }
--ThisRandomString
Content-type: image/gif
{ GIF Data for the second frame }
    .
    .
    .
```

```
--ThisRandomString
Content-type: image/gif
{ GIF Data for the last frame }
--ThisRandomString--
```

The final two dashes (--) appended to the boundary string signal that the last block has been sent and the connect can be closed. No matter how slow the loop is, as long as the reader doesn't interfere, the browser will keep the connection open, waiting patiently for each block of data to be sent to replace the previous one.

PERSISTENT HTTP COOKIES

Cookies are another Netscape enhancement. This one addresses the general problem inherent in the Web's architecture—servers have no memory. That is, without extensive programming on the server to gather and store information about each reader and what they are doing at any given time, it is very difficult to tie Web pages together into an application. On the Web, a server simply handles requests from readers who, once they get the page they want, go away. With an online service, the situation is the opposite—the service knows who you are, has your billing information, and is paying attention to every key you hit. An online service is a better environment for integrated applications.

Enter cookies. Netscape says they decided to call them "cookies" for no good reason whatsoever. A cookie (think of the fortune kind) is a packet of arbitrary information sent to the browser by a server-side script. A cookie has an expiration date and the browser will hang onto that cookie until it expires. The cookie also has a list of URLs (usually scripts), and the browser will send the contents of the cookie should the reader link to an URL in that list.

Say you visit a page that contains a form, enter some information, check some boxes, and click the submit button. The script processing the information from the form sends a cookie back to the browser. The cookie contains information from the form as a set of strings in the format keyword=value, where the keywords are the names of the form fields and the values are what you typed in and selected. The script can include additional information in the cookie, such as a temporary customer id. After some time, but before the expiration date of the cookie, you visit a second page that also has a form, which you fill out and submit to a script whose URL is in the list of URLs associated with the cookie. The browser will send the cookie to the script in the HTTP header, giving this second script access to all the information you entered into the first form, and more. All this happens without the server having to do any work at all to store that information.

This is an important enhancement. For example, imagine a college registration system, with each department and class having its own page on the Web. As you select your courses by selecting items from forms on the pages, server scripts can spot conflicts and check availability. You are free to rearrange your course schedule as often as you like because the server does as little work as possible until you reach the cashier's page and provide payment.

Likewise, if you visit a cybermall, the cookies can be the items in your "shopping basket" that you carry from department to department before you get to the "checkout" page. You can freely leave the store (go to WebLouvre or *Hot-Wired,* or check out a manufacturer's site, for example) and return days later to continue shopping—without needing a password!

For the complete syntax of HTTP cookies, see Netscape's description at: http://www.netscape.com/newsref/std/cookie_spec.html.

APPLETS—JAVA

A lot of people are very excited about Java, Sun Microsystem's programming language for distributed applications, and the HotJava browser. Unfortunately, many of the pieces needed to put Java into play on the Web are still in beta testing. Version 2.0 of Netscape Navigator has Java support for some operating systems. At the time of this writing, however, Netscape 2.0 is in beta and the Java support is very buggy. Still the excitement continues to grow.

What's so wonderful about Java? A lot: On a Web page, Java-enabled browsers can play inline sounds when a page loads, or supply ambient music for a page. A Java browser can play real-time video and generate simple animations. A Java browser should be able to do most anything an application program can do on your computer, including communicating over the Internet. Java, however, is much more than just the next hot Web browser. Java is a programming language for distributed applications. Netscape and Microsoft are also working on such languages. This general description should also apply to those companys' products.

Without Java the Web is a space filled with data objects—pages, images, sound clips, and so on. These objects can either be static as files waiting to be downloaded, or dynamically generated by CGI scripts. Still, HTTP is only designed for moving data objects from here to there.

With Java, objects traversing the Web can carry with them the necessary code for the object to interact with the reader. Such enhanced objects are called applets. Applets are platform-independent. A Java program will run equally well on any computer that has a Java-enabled browser. Java programs are compressed to a compact format called byte code, which is interpreted and executed on the fly by a Java-enabled browser.

Today, when a new data type is introduced to the Web—Adobe Acrobat and Real Audio are recent examples—it takes some time before enough readers have downloaded the helper application for that data type before it is worthwhile for authors to make use of it.

There are three parts to the Java environment: a Java-enabled Web browser, a Java compiler to turn Java source code into byte code, and a Java interpreter to test and run stand-alone Java programs. Java is an object-oriented programming (OOP) language, and the process of writing and testing a Java applet is the same as that of C++ programs. Most of the resources for learning the language and the environment are listed on Sun's Java page at: <http://java.sun.com/>. Some other Java development resources are listed in Appendix B.

Applets are added to Web pages with the <APPLET></APPLET> tags, which describe the applet: its height and width, and any parameters. When a Java-enabled browser encounters an APPLET tag, it downloads the code for the applet and executes it. Here, for example, is the HTML to call a simple applet that will play in a 300 × 200 pixel rectangle:

```
<APPLET CODE="appname.class" WIDTH=300 HEIGHT=200></APPLET>
```

The CODE argument identifies the applet with a relative URL. In this example, the applet appname.class is in the same directory as the Web page that calls it. The APPLET tag is not an HTML structural element. No paragraph breaks are implied either before or after the applet. Like images and figures, an applet appears inline with other content and markup. In fact, most of the attributes and values that are used with the IMAGE and FIGURE tags such as ALIGN, VALIGN, HSPACE, VSPACE, and ALT can be used in the APPLET tag.

An applet can be on a different server from that of the referring page even though relative addressing must be used in the CODE attribute. The CODE-BASE attribute can be used to provide a base URL for the applet as in:

```
<APPLET CODE="appname.class"
BASECODE="http://applets_R_us.com/classes/"
WIDTH=300 HEIGHT=200>
</APPLET>
```

Any content that appears between the starting and ending APPLET tags is considered "alternate content." Alternate content can contain any HTML elements, including images and figures. When read by a Java-enabled browser, it will be ignored. When the APPLET tags are read by a browser that is not Java-aware, the APPLET tags will be ignored.

A well-designed Java applet will be configurable with a set of parameters controlling most of its important aspects. This allows the HTML author to customize an applet without having to edit and recompile any Java code. Since each applet recognizes a different set of applet parameters, they are specified with <PARAM> tags placed just after the beginning <APPLET> tag and before any alternate content. Each PARAM tag has NAME and VALUE attributes whose values are specific to the applet called. For example, a generalized applet that provides animation by repeatedly looping through a set of images might be written with <PARAM> tags that specify the image set and timings:

```
<APPLET CODE="animator.class" WIDTH=144 HEIGHT=216>
<PARAM NAME="images" VALUE=8>
<PARAM NAME="frameset" VALUE="duke">
<PARAM NAME="pause" VALUE=1000>
<IMG SRC="duke.gif" ALT="Sun's Java mascot, Duke">
</APPLET>
```

In the above HTML, PARAM tags stipulate the number of images in the animation, the location of the images, and how many milliseconds the animator applet should pause between frames. An image of Duke, Sun's rather strange-looking Java mascot, is the alternate content in this example.

Java is a general programming language, not just a Web scripting language. Java will let you do just about anything you can do with a traditional programming language like C++. In fact, Java is very similar to C, although much easier to use and cleaner in design. Platform-independent and distributed on the Web, Java might well become tomorrow's language of choice for personal programming.

HTML Examples

Example 1—A personal home page

Example 2—A tutorial page

Example 3—A small organization's home page

Example 4—A large organization's home page

Example 5—A page of Internet resources

Example 6—A page covering a subject field

In this chapter I've collected a number of examples of World Wide
Web pages. Each example includes a presentation and discussion of
the HTML source for the example Web page followed by a reproduction of the page. The examples were chosen with variety in mind to let you
know what you can do with HTML and your information. Not all of the
pages represent the best HTML use. That's fine. This is the work of busy people, motivated by the desire to make their information public with tools that
are still evolving. I'll point out instances of poor (in my opinion) HTML use
here and there, and I hope the authors won't think I'm being judgmental. I've
written a zillion lines of code over the years and would hate to have anyone
judge my work on such a small sample.

These example pages are still evolving. What are presented here are snap-
shots of pages at a particular point in late 1995. I'm providing the URLs of the
example pages with no guarantee that they will continue to be valid, and cer-
tainly no guarantee that the pages seen on the Web at those addresses will be
the same as those presented here. If they are, you'll probably see improvements.

EXAMPLE 1—A PERSONAL HOME PAGE

This example is the home page of Gary Welz. When the first edition of this book
was published Gary's home page was at <http://found.cs.nyu.edu/found.a/CAT/
misc/welz/>. Gary's Webspace has grown considerably and now that URL points
to an index of the many pages in his webspace. What used to be at that URL is
now at: <http://found.cs.nyu.edu/found.a/CAT/misc/welz/welzresume.html>

and is the HTML source in this example. The page is a combination of résumé and work-summary. The list of Gary's favorite links which used to be part of his home page is now at <http://found.cs.nyu.edu/found.a/CAT/misc/welz/sites.html>. I like this page because Gary has worked on many interesting Web projects all of which are linked to this page.

The page begins with a <BODY> tag setting the background color to white (#FFFFFF) followed by a black-and-white image of Gary, which loads quickly on a slow link (good idea). The image is embedded in the level 1 heading and is placed so that the middle of the image is aligned with the rest of the heading text. Following that are three short address elements providing Gary's postal and electronic mail addresses. These address elements could have easily been coded as a single address block with two-line break tags, for example

```
<address>165 Bennett Ave #4-M<br>
New York, NY 10040<br>
email: gary@setn.org</address>
```

The remainder of the page is a series of short sections each introduced by a level 4 heading. There are really no major divisions of this page and that is reflected in the lack of any level 2 or 3 headings. There's a lot of information on this page neatly organized by unordered lists and short narative paragraphs. Other than setting the background color, this page uses no HTML3 features and should display uniformly over the widest range of browsers. I have very few suggestions for this HTML code, but here they are: First, the author should have used citation tags (<CITE></CITE>) around the name of publications in the text instead of italic tags (<I></I>). Second, many of the URLs in the HTML source are not enclosed in double quotation marks. They really should be. And finally, paragraph tags are neither required nor recommended before other HTML structural elements such as headings and lists.

```
<HTML>
<HEAD>
<TITLE>Gary Welz: Resume</TITLE>
</HEAD>

<BODY bgcolor="#FFFFFF">

<H1><IMG ALIGN = middle SRC = gary2.gif> Gary Welz</H1>

<address>165 Bennett Ave #4-M</address>
```

EXAMPLE 1—A PERSONAL HOME PAGE   **127**

```
<address>New York, NY 10040</address>
<address>email: gary@setn.org</address>
<P>
<H4>Recent Activity:</H4>
```

For the past two years I have been an Internet Consultant and New Media journalist. My clients have included the New York Public Library, the Association for Computing Machinery, Viacom New Media and Conde' Nast New Media. I've published articles in such publications as `<I>Internet World</I>`, `<I>Internetmci</I>`, `<I>The X Advisor</I>` and ACM `<I>Interactions</I>`. My current position is Production Manager and Webmaster for `<I>New Jersey Online</I>`, an electronic publication of Newhouse New Media.

```
<P>
<H4>Education:</H4>
<UL>
<LI>1976 B.A. Philosophy & Mathematics, Bedford College, Univ., of
London, London, England.
<LI>1977 M. Sc. Mathematics, Bedford College, Univ. of London, London,
England.
</UL>

<H4>Teaching:</H4>
<UL>
<LI>1995 Taught staff of the New York Public Library how to gather
information on the Internet and author documents in Hypertext Markup
Language.
<LI>1994 Instructor at the CUNY Computer Center, teaching faculty and
staff how to gather information on the Internet and author documents in
Hypertext Markup Language.
<LI>1982-1994  Adjunct Lecturer in Mathematics at John Jay College, and
Herbert H. Lehman College of the City University of New York.</UL>

<H4>Internet Sites Developed or Worked On</H4>
<UL>
<LI><A HREF="index.html">My WWW home page</A>
<LI><A HREF="http://www.nj.com">New Jersey Online</A>, a publication of
Newhouse New Media
<LI><A HREF="http://www.epicurious.com">Epicurious</A>, a publication
of Conde' Nast New Media
```

```
<A HREF=http://www.nypl.org/research/sibl/index.html>Science, Industry
and Business Library Home Page</A> SIBL is a division of the New York
Public Library.
<LI><A HREF=http://math240.lehman.cuny.edu/art/>Breaking Out (of the
Virtual Closet)</A>, a WWW art project designed for artist Douglas
Davis at the Lehman College Art Gallery.
<LI><A
HREF=http://bang.lanl.gov/video/stv/arshtml/lanlarstitle.html>The Art
of Renaissance Science:  Galileo and Perspective</A>, a hypermedia
essay created with Prof. Joseph W. Dauben of the CUNY Computer Center
as a protype WWW journal article.
<LI><A HREF=http://www.service.com/stv/setncall.html>Science and
Engineering Television Network Call for Participation</A> and <A
HREF=http://www.service.com/stv/survey.html>Survey</A>
<LI><A HREF=http://www.service.com/stv/>A Science Television Company
WWW advertisement</A></UL>

<H4>Internet Media Related Publications:</H4>
<UL>
<LI><A
HREF="http://www.crispzine.com/contents/currents/radio.html">Radio on
the Net</A> in Crisp, an new electronic magazine.
<LI><A HREF="http://landru.unx.com/DD/advisor/TOC/v1n5TOC.shtml">Audio
and Radio on on the Net</A> <I>The X Advisor</I>, October, 1995.  This
will take you to the Table of Contents.  Scroll down to my column,
called <I>Peripheral Visions</I>.  If you haven't already subscribed to
<I>The X Advisor</I> you will have to  do so by filling out a form.
Subscribing is free and instantaneous.
<LI><A
HREF="http://landru.unx.com/DD/advisor/TOC/v1n4TOC.shtml">Internet
Telephony</A> <I>The X Advisor</I>, September, 1995.  This will take
you to the Table of Contents.  Scroll down to my column, called
<I>Peripheral Visions</I>.  If you haven't already subscribed to <I>The
X Advisor</I> you will have to  do so by filling out a form.
Subscribing is free and instantaneous.
<LI><A HREF="http://landru.unx.com/DD/advisor/TOC/v1n3TOC.shtml">Phase
Transition:  The Online Medium Comes of Age</A> <I>The X Advisor</I>,
August, 1995.  This will take you to the Table of Contents.  Scroll
down to my column, called <I>Peripheral Visions</I>.  If you haven't
```

EXAMPLE 1—A PERSONAL HOME PAGE **129**

already subscribed to <I>The X Advisor</I> you will have to do so by
filling out a form. Subscribing is free and instantaneous.
<LI><A
HREF="http://landru.unx.com/DD/advisor/docs/jul95/welz.genome0.shtml">Is
a Genome Like a Computer Program?</A>, <I>The X Advisor</I>, July,
1995. If you haven't already subscribed to <I>The X Advisor</I> you
will have to access the <A
HREF="http://landru.unx.com/DD/advisor/TOC/v1n2TOC.shtml">The X Advisor
Issue #2 Table of Contents page</A> and subscribed by filling out a
form. Subscribing is free and instantaneous. Then you'll be able to
view the article in my monthly column which is called "Peripheral
Visions."
<LI><A HREF="http://pubs.iworld.com/iw-online/Jun95/feat36.htm">New
Deals</A>,<I> Internet World</I>, June 1995.
<LI><A
HREF="http://landru.unx.com/DD/advisor/docs/jun95/jun95.gwelz.shtml">
Zooming Through Information Space on Pad++</A>, <I>The X Advisor</I>,
June 1995.   Again, if you have not subscribed to <I>The X Advisor</I>
you will have to do so by accessing <A
HREF="http://landru.unx.com/DD/advisor/TOC/v1n1TOC.shtml">The X Advisor
Issue #1 Table of Contents page</A> and subscribed by filling out a
form.   Then you'll be able to view the article in my monthly column
which is called "Peripheral Visions."
<LI>Through the Electronic Veil: Acting and Interacting in Virtual
Worlds, <I>Net Editors, internetMCI</I>, April 28, 1995.
<LI><A HREF="http://pubs.iworld.com/iw-online/May95/feat48.htm">Cyber
Spiels: A tour of web ads online & Career Connections: Job seeking on
the net</A>, <I>Internet World</I>, May 1995.
<LI><A HREF="http://pubs.iworld.com/iw-online/Mar95/feat30.htm">New
Dimensions: a Multimedia Revolution is Unfolding on the Net</A>,
<I>Internet World</I>, March 1995
<LI><A HREF=http://found.cs.nyu.edu/found.a/CAT/misc/welz/articles/
interact.html>Hypermedia, Multimedia and Television on the Internet:
Some of the best tools in life are free</A>, <I>Interactions</I>, July
1994
<LI><A HREF=http://found.cs.nyu.edu/found.a/CAT/misc/welz/articles/
mediabusiness.html>Abstract of: The Media Business on the WWW</A>, 2nd
International WWW Conference, October 1994.
<LI><A HREF=http://www.ncsa.uiuc.edu/SDG/IT94/Proceedings/ComEc/welz/

welzwwwconf.html>The Media Business on the WWW</A>, 2nd International
WWW Conference, October 1994. (An updated version of this paper
appeared in the June '95 issue of <I>The X Journal</I>.)
<LI><A HREF=http://found.cs.nyu.edu/found.a/CAT/misc/welz/articles/
internettv.html>Television on the Internet - Scientific Publishing in a
New Medium</A>, Proceedings of the 7th Conference and General Assembly
of the International Federation of Science Editors, July 1993.
</UL>

<H4>Major Project:</H4>
Developed a proposal for the creation of a television network for
scientists and engineers with grants totaling nearly $100,000 from the
Alfred P. Sloan Foundation. This led to the founding of the <A
HREF=http://found.cs.nyu.edu/found.a/CAT/misc/welz/setn/>Science and
Engineering Television Network, Inc.</A> a non-profit corporation
supported by the Association for Computing Machinery, the American
Physical Society and other professional societies.<P>

<H4>Video Producing and Directing:</H4>
1989-Present Founder of the Science Television Company, a private sole
proprietorship in the business of producing videotapes for scientists.
These tapes are currently distributed by the Association for Computing
Machinery, the American Mathematical Society and others. Titles
include: <P>
<UL>
<LI><A HREF=http://www.service.com/stv/nms.html>Natural Minimal
Surfaces via Theory and Computation</A> with Prof. David Hoffman
<LI><A HREF=http://www.service.com/stv/cfd.html>Chaos, Fractals and
Dynamics</A> and <A
HREF=http://www.service.com/stv/ttc.html>Transition to Chaos</A> with
Prof. Robert L. Devaney
<LI><A HREF=http://www.service.com/stv/bcm.html>The Beauty and
Complexity of the Mandelbrot Set</A> with Prof. John H. Hubbard
<LI><A HREF=http://www.service.com/stv/im.html>Introducing
Mathematica</A> with Stephen Wolfram
<LI><A HREF=http://www.service.com/stv/ars.html>The Art of Renaissance
Science</A> with Joseph W. Dauben. </UL><P>

EXAMPLE 1—A PERSONAL HOME PAGE   **131**

These tapes are currently being viewed in digital form at <A
HREF=http://bang.lanl.gov/video/>Los Alamos National Laboratory</A>
where they are being used in an experimental LAN video project.<P>

1994 - Contracted by the Courant Institute of NYU and the Mathematical
Science Research Institute in Berkeley, CA to produce and direct a
video concerning mathematics research entitled <I>Forced Lattice
Vibrations</I> featuring Prof. Percy Deift of NYU and others. <P>

<H4>A bibliography of articles about my work:</H4>
<UL>
<LI>WebFeats: Surfs Up on the Cyber Sea, John Strasbaugh, <I>The New
York Press</I> January 11, 1995
<LI><A
HREF=http://found.cs.nyu.edu/found.a/CAT/misc/welz/setn/elink.html>
Internet Science Gets Hip</A>, <I>Electronic Link Magazine</I>,
June/July '94
<LI><A
HREF=http://found.cs.nyu.edu/found.a/CAT/misc/welz/setn/macweek.html>
Digital Publications Arriving</A>, <I>MacWeek</I>, October 18, 1993
<LI><A
HREF=http://found.cs.nyu.edu/found.a/CAT/misc/welz/setn/scicomm.html>
Information Technology</A>, <I>Science Communication</I>, January 1993
<LI><A
HREF=http://found.cs.nyu.edu/found.a/CAT/misc/welz/setn/setnpress.html
#Nature>Science Goes Video</A>, Peter Aldhous, <I>Nature</I>, August 8,
1991
<LI><A
HREF=http://found.cs.nyu.edu/found.a/CAT/misc/welz/setn/setnpress.html
#Science>Science Television: Colleagues on Cable</A>, Marcia Barinaga,
<I>Science</I>, March 15, 1991
<LI><A
HREF=http://found.cs.nyu.edu/found.a/CAT/misc/welz/setn/setnpress.html
#Guardian>Thinking Big on the Small Screen</A>, Keith Devlin, <I>The
Guardian</I>, June 14, 1990
</UL><P>

</BODY>
</HTML>

Figure 7.1 shows how the Web page generated by this HTML code will look displayed and printed using Netscape. Oh, one more criticism, which I illustrate with the old saying *It's a long cow that has no tail*: This page needs an ending; something to balance the visual weight of the image and heading that began the page, and to provide a final focus for its content.

Gary Welz

165 Bennett Ave #4-M
New York, NY 10040
email: gary@setn.org

Recent Activity:

For the past two years I have been an Internet Consultant and New Media journalist. My clients have included the New York Public Library, the Association for Computing Machinery, Viacom New Media and Conde' Nast New Media. I've published articles in such publications as *Internet World*, *Internetmci*, *The X Advisor* and ACM *Interactions*. My current position is Production Manager and Webmaster for *New Jersey Online*, an electronic publication of Newhouse New Media.

Education:

- 1976 B.A. Philosophy & Mathematics, Bedford College, Univ., of London, London, England.
- 1977 M. Sc. Mathematics, Bedford College, Univ. of London, London, England.

Teaching:

- 1995 Taught staff of the New York Public Library how to gather information on the Internet and author documents in Hypertext Markup Language.
- 1994 Instructor at the CUNY Computer Center, teaching faculty and staff how to gather information on the Internet and author documents in Hypertext Markup Language.
- 1982-1994 Adjunct Lecturer in Mathematics at John Jay College, and Herbert H. Lehman College of the City University of New York.

Internet Sites Developed or Worked On

- My WWW home page
- New Jersey Online, a publication of Newhouse New Media
- Epicurious, a publication of Conde' Nast New Media Science, Industry and Business Library Home Page SIBL is a division of the New York Public Library.
- Breaking Out (of the Virtual Closet), a WWW art project designed for artist Douglas Davis at the Lehman College Art Gallery.
- The Art of Renaissance Science: Galileo and Perspective, a hypermedia essay created with Prof. Joseph W. Dauben of the CUNY Computer Center as a protype WWW journal article.
- Science and Engineering Television Network Call for Participation and Survey
- A Science Television Company WWW advertisement

Internet Media Related Publications:

- Radio on the Net in Crisp, an new electronic magazine.

Figure 7.1: Gary Welz's home page

EXAMPLE 1—A PERSONAL HOME PAGE **133**

- Audio and Radio on on the Net *The X Advisor*, October, 1995. This will take you to the Table of Contents. Scroll down to my column, called *Peripheral Visions*. If you haven't already subscribed to *The X Advisor* you will have to do so by filling out a form. Subscribing is free and instantaneous.
- Internet Telephony *The X Advisor*, September, 1995. This will take you to the Table of Contents. Scroll down to my column, called *Peripheral Visions*. If you haven't already subscribed to *The X Advisor* you will have to do so by filling out a form. Subscribing is free and instantaneous.
- Phase Transition: The Online Medium Comes of Age *The X Advisor*, August, 1995. This will take you to the Table of Contents. Scroll down to my column, called *Peripheral Visions*. If you haven't already subscribed to *The X Advisor* you will have to do so by filling out a form. Subscribing is free and instantaneous.
- Is a Genome Like a Computer Program?, *The X Advisor*, July, 1995. If you haven't already subscribed to *The X Advisor* you will have to access the The X Advisor Issue #2 Table of Contents page and subscribed by filling out a form. Subscribing is free and instantaneous. Then you'll be able to view the article in my monthly column which is called "Peripheral Visions."
- New Deals, *Internet World*, June 1995.
- Zooming Through Information Space on Pad++, *The X Advisor*, June 1995. Again, if you have not subscribed to *The X Advisor* you will have to do so by accessing The X Advisor Issue #1 Table of Contents page and subscribed by filling out a form. Then you'll be able to view the article in my monthly column which is called "Peripheral Visions."
- Through the Electronic Veil: Acting and Interacting in Virtual Worlds, *Net Editors, internetMCI*, April 28, 1995.
- Cyber Spiels: A tour of web ads online & Career Connections: Job seeking on the net, *Internet World*, May 1995.
- New Dimensions: a Multimedia Revolution is Unfolding on the Net, *Internet World*, March 1995
- Hypermedia, Multimedia and Television on the Internet: Some of the best tools in life are free, *Interactions*, July 1994
- Abstract of: The Media Business on the WWW, 2nd International WWW Conference, October 1994.
- The Media Business on the WWW, 2nd International WWW Conference, October 1994. (An updated version of this paper appeared in the June '95 issue of *The X Journal*.)
- Television on the Internet - Scientific Publishing in a New Medium, Proceedings of the 7th Conference and General Assembly of the International Federation of Science Editors, July 1993.

Major Project:

Developed a proposal for the creation of a television network for scientists and engineers with grants totaling nearly $100,000 from the Alfred P. Sloan Foundation. This led to the founding of the Science and Engineering Television Network, Inc. a non-profit corporation supported by the Association for Computing Machinery, the American Physical Society and other professional societies.

Video Producing and Directing:

1989-Present Founder of the Science Television Company, a private sole proprietorship in the business of producing videotapes for scientists. These tapes are currently distributed by the Association for Computing Machinery, the American Mathematical Society and others. Titles include:

- Natural Minimal Surfaces via Theory and Computation with Prof. David Hoffman
- Chaos, Fractals and Dynamics and Transition to Chaos with Prof. Robert L. Devaney
- The Beauty and Complexity of the Mandelbrot Set with Prof. John H. Hubbard
- Introducing Mathematica with Stephen Wolfram
- The Art of Renaissance Science with Joseph W. Dauben.

These tapes are currently being viewed in digital form at Los Alamos National Laboratory where they are being used in an experimental LAN video project.

1994 - Contracted by the Courant Institute of NYU and the Mathematical Science Research Institute in Berkeley, CA to produce and direct a video concerning mathematics research entitled *Forced Lattice Vibrations* featuring Prof. Percy Deift of NYU and others.

A bibliography of articles about my work:

- WebFeats: Surfs Up on the Cyber Sea, John Strasbaugh, *The New York Press* January 11, 1995
- Internet Science Gets Hip, *Electronic Link Magazine*, June/July '94
- Digital Publications Arriving, *MacWeek*, October 18, 1993
- Information Technology, *Science Communication*, January 1993
- Science Goes Video, Peter Aldhous, *Nature*, August 8, 1991
- Science Television: Colleagues on Cable, Marcia Barinaga, *Science*, March 15, 1991
- Thinking Big on the Small Screen, Keith Devlin, *The Guardian*, June 14, 1990

Figure 7.1: Gary Welz's home page (continued)

EXAMPLE 2—A TUTORIAL PAGE

I was surfing my publisher's pages when I found this wonderful tutorial on how to create a home page. There are dozens of pages on the Web that try to explain how to put together Web pages. This is the best one I've seen. It's written by Anna Smith of *ComputerLife UK* magazine and I'm pleased to be able to include it here. It's especially good for those of you who have bought this book (or maybe it was given to you) but who don't really want to read it. The pages's URL is <http://www.ziff.com/~clifeuk/issues/9506/howto01.html>. I've edited the HTML only for length, removing the last three sections.

The <BODY> tag includes a BACKGROUND attribute pointing to an image to be used as the background pattern. For practical reasons, the reproduction of the page for this example does not show the background pattern, which is too bad. It's a very nice one based on the logo image, *ComputerLife*, at the top of the page, in pink and purple. The URL for the GIF file references it from the root directory of the server. We can infer from this URL that the Web server at ziff.com hosts several user Websites. This particular page belongs to *ComputerLife UK*'s userid, clifeuk. The background graphic is up a couple directory levels from the HTML page's location, so it's a lot cleaner to address it from the root. If this page is later archived at a different level of the server, the link will still work.

The first element on the page is *ComputerLife*'s logo image. The image tag pre-specifies the size of the image for better performance; the VSPACE and HSPACE attributes, however, are not needed here. They only apply when text flow is specified by giving the ALIGN attribute a value of "right" or "left." This image tag and the one at the end of the page include an ALT attribute providing descriptions of the images for readers who don't have their browsers set to automatically load images. Including the ALT tag is a good habit; it has the added advantage of documenting the image tags in your HTML source.

This Web work is nicely designed. It was *built* from a magazine article rather than *converted* from one. After the *ComputerLife* logo is a level 1 heading with the title of the page followed by a short, clear introduction and a table of contents implemented as an unordered list. The introduction and the contents are given a little punch by enclosing them in font tags specifying that a font size one larger than normal should be used to render these elements. The links in the table of contents are all to anchors within this same page. Although this work could have been implemented as several Web pages—one per section—there really isn't a good reason to do the extra work. Because images are used sparingly, it loads fast enough on slow links and has the advantage of printing out in one piece.

EXAMPLE 2—A TUTORIAL PAGE   **135**

After the contents is a more formal introductory section of three paragraphs separated from other page elements with horizontal rules. In writing a page like this today, we might enclose this three-paragraph section in division tags with a class attribute, for example, <DIV CLASS="intro"> ... </DIV>, in order to do something interesting with it later.

```
<HTML>
<HEAD>
<TITLE>
Computer Life UK gets you online
</TITLE>
<!--Computer Life Issue 2 Web Pages May 1995-->
</HEAD>

<BODY BACKGROUND="/~clifeuk/graphics/clbg1.jpg">
<IMG WIDTH="166" HEIGHT="38" VSPACE="0" HSPACE="0"
SRC="/~clifeuk/graphics/cluklog2.gif" ALT="Computer Life UK logo">
<H1>Create your own home pages</H1>
<FONT SIZE="+1">
Become at one with the Internet by setting up your own World Wide Web
pages. We show you how. <EM>by Anna Smith</EM>
<UL>
<LI><A HREF="#step1">Step 1</A> Design a template
<LI><A HREF="#step2">Step 2</A> Add the <A HREF="#words">words,</A> <A
HREF="#pics">pictures,</A> and <A HREF="#links">links</A>
<LI><A HREF="#pub">Publish your page</A>
<LI><A HREF="#more">You want more!?</A>
<LI><A HREF="#tricks">Party Tricks</A>
<LI><A HREF="#donts">Don't do this.. at all</A>
<LI><A HREF="#acalert">Acronym Alert</A>
</UL>
</FONT>

<HR>

Writing your own home pages will give you 15 minutes of fame and
stardom -
and a healthy respect for the annoying problems that can crop up when
you create them. We'll walk you through the basics of how to create a
text file that will turn into an HTML file when viewed using a browser
```

```
such as Netscape.

<P>
Ever wondered why some Web pages have those embarrassing line breaks or
why not every page is full of graphics? Well, Web pages, written in the
text-based browser language known as HTML, can be more than a little
tricky to get just right. However, there is a variety of new shareware
and commercial packages on the market which make it easier. We've
included two software programs on the CD-ROM:
<A HREF="http://pringle.mta.ca/~peterc/">HTMLed</A> and
<A
HREF="http://www.microsoft.com/pages/deskapps/word/ia/default.htm">Micro
soft Word 6.0's Internet Assistant.</A>

<P>
Braver souls can write HTML pages using any text editor (including
Windows Notepad) and by saving it as a TXT file, just as long as you
follow certain basic guidelines. Although the more sophisticated
programs automate the process, it's helpful to understand the basics of
HTML design when you set out to create your own pages.
<HR>
```

The rest of the content of the page is divided into sections each beginning
with a level 2 heading. Each heading is given a name with an anchor tag which
is referenced in the table of contents at the top of the page. The ID attribute
could also be used, added to the heading tag, but, when this page was written
in mid-1995, not many browsers supported this attribute. Anna has adopted
the convention of strongly emphasizing all HTML code to distinguish it from
the narrative text. To display the markup characters &, <, and >, she is using
character entities providing the ASCII index of these characters, for example,
&#60 for the less than sign and &#62 for the greater than sign.

```
<H2><A NAME="step1">Step 1: Design a template</A></H2>
There are certain tags (instructions to a hypertext browser) that you
must include in your Web page. It's easiest to put these in first as the
bones of your template. To begin, open a file using one of the packages
we've included on the CD-ROM or a basic text editor and save the file
with an HTM extension. Then add the following text.
<P>
<STRONG>&#60;HTML&#62;</STRONG><BR>
```

EXAMPLE 2—A TUTORIAL PAGE **137**

The very first tag. This tells the browser that a hypertext page is coming up. If the tag's not there, the browser will display anything that follows as plain text, including all other tags.
<P>
<STRONG><HEAD></STRONG>
The head of a hypertext page contains information about it: its title and any version/ownership info.
<P>
<STRONG><TITLE></STRONG>
The title of your page as browsers will see it. The TITLE element always sits between the <STRONG><HEAD></STRONG> and <STRONG></HEAD></STRONG> tags and must be plain text only.
<P>
<STRONG></TITLE></STRONG>
Closes the title part of the page.
<P>
<STRONG><!--Your comment here--></STRONG>
Comment tags. Put the date here, for example. Comments aren't shown on screen.
<P>
<STRONG></HEAD></STRONG>
Closes the head part of your page. Now you can go on to the fun bit!
<P>
<STRONG><BODY></STRONG>
The start tag of the area where you put text, pictures, sound files, and pointers to other interesting parts of the Web. Be bold, be smart, be creative! Presentation is crucial, so make your pages a pleasure for others to read.
<P>
<STRONG><HR></STRONG>
This optional tag displays a horizontal rule across the page. Use it as a visual cue that this is the end of the page. Put your e-mail address under the rule.
<P>
<STRONG></BODY></STRONG>
Closes the body area.
<P>
<STRONG></HTML></STRONG>
The very last tag. It closes your hypertext page.

```
<HR>
<H2><A NAME="step2">Step 2: Add the words, pictures and links</A></H2>
<STRONG><A NAME="words">Headings</A></STRONG><BR>
It's considered good hypertext practice to make the first element after
the opening &#60;BODY&#62; tag a heading, announcing what your page is
about.
<P>
There are six levels of heading, the first of which produces large, bold
lettering, with space above and below. Experiment with your HTML editor
and various browsers to see what they look like. The tag for a level one
heading looks like this:
<P>
<STRONG>&#60;H1&#62;</STRONG><BR>
<H1>This is a first level heading</H1>
<STRONG>&#60;/H1&#62;</STRONG>
<P>
I've tagged the sentence "This is a first level heading" so you can see
what a level one heading looks like on your browser.
<P>
<STRONG>Text</STRONG><BR>
Any text that is not enclosed within tags is shown on screen as plain
text. All HTML documents must be saved as plain ASCII files. Browsers
recognise nothing but word-breaks--they won't see the line and
paragraph breaks generated by your word processor. You must specify
exactly where you want each paragraph to break. Line width changes
according to the size of the window your reader has chosen on her
browser.
<P>
Be kind to your readers and keep paragraphs short--a huge block of
unbroken text is off-putting.
<P>
To break a line, type
<STRONG>&#60;BR&#62;</STRONG><BR>
The next line starts immediately below.
<P>
For a paragraph break, type
<STRONG>&#60;P&#62;</STRONG>
<P>
This inserts a space between the lines.
```

Example 2—A tutorial page **139**

```
<P>
You may want to emphasise a line or a word. There are two basic
attribute tags. The first is
<P>
<STRONG>&#60;STRONG&#62;</STRONG><BR>
<STRONG>Usually makes your text look bold.</STRONG><BR>
<STRONG>&#60;/STRONG&#62;</STRONG>
<P>
And the other is
<P>
<STRONG>&#60;EM&#62;</STRONG><BR>
<EM>Short for "emphasised". Usually makes your text look
italic.</EM><BR>
<STRONG>&#60;/EM&#62;</STRONG>
<HR>
<H2><A NAME="pics">Pictures</A></H2>
Pictures should be in GIF or JPEG formats. There are programs available
for downloading which will convert PC graphics into whichever of these
two
you prefer. JPEGs tend to compress smaller than GIFs (especially with
large images), but use a "lossy" algorithm that degrades image quality.
Best thing to do is experiment and see how your graphics look in your
browser.
<P>
The HTML tag for inserting a picture is:
<P>
<STRONG>&#60;IMG SRC=yourpic.gif ALT="Picture of a
whatever"&#62;</STRONG>
<P>
Obviously replace <STRONG>'yourpic.gif'</STRONG> with the actual name
of your graphics file. The ALT tag displays text which describes your
picture. It is a courtesy for the benefit of text-only browser users.
<HR>
<H2><A NAME="links">Linking to other Web pages</A></H2>
If your home page is all about "Star Trek," for example, you'll want to
tell other fans where more ST goodies can be found. You do this with
what HTML calls an "anchor"--it's the blue underlined text that you
click on to do something or go somewhere. Graphics can be anchors too.
This is the tag you use:
```

```
<P>
<STRONG>&#60;A
HREF="http://www.somewhere.co.uk/brilliant_startrek_site.html"&#62;</STR
ONG><BR>
Click here for a brilliant Star Trek site!<BR>
<STRONG>&#60;/A&#62;</STRONG>
<P>
The text between the double quotes is the URL of the Web page you want
people to visit. You can also link to FTP sites and newsgroups. Because
URLs are case-sensitive, be careful to type them correctly--some use
all lower-case letters, some include capital letters. You can also use
them to link to additional pages that you create, giving your home page
more depth.
<HR>
<H2><A NAME="pub">Publishing Your Page</A></H2>
When you have finished your files, contact your Internet provider for
information on how to upload them. It varies from company to company,
but many providers are offering free space as part of their sign up
offers.
<HR>
```

Like any good tutorial, this page assumes that it has only whetted the appetite and provides a section of further references for its readers. Following that the work closes nicely with a short bio of the author, a link back to the Webspace's home page in button and text, a copyright notice and, finally, a signature in an address block. The only thing that's missing is a timestamp so the reader knows how current the information is. Updated for HTML3, the bio and copyright paragraphs would use paragraph containers with CLASS attributes to take advantage of styles.

```
<H2><A NAME="more">You want more!?</a></H2>
If you want more hints and tips, you can of course find these on the
Web itself. Here are a few places to start you off:
<P>
<A HREF="http://www.charm.net/~web/Vlib.html">The World Wide Web
Virtual Library</A> is a cornucopia of links to everything you need to
know about making World Wide Web pages. Explore thoroughly!
<P>
The <a href="http://www.charm.net/~web/Vlib/Providers/HTML.html">Virtual
Library's HTML index</A> is where you download The Beginner's Guide to
```

Example 2—A tutorial page **141**

```
HTML and other information about HTML editing.
<P>
Some nice people at Rutgers University have a <A HREF="http://www-
ns.rutgers.edu/doc-images">collection of public domain graphics</A> to
use in your documents.
<P>
The <A HREF="http://gnn.com/gnn/netizens/construction.html">Home Page
Construction Kit</A> shows you how to create an HTML file and put the
file on a Web server.
<HR>
```
   [content removed]
```
<HR>
Anna Smith - <A HREF="mailto:mjau@henry.demon.co.uk">
mjau@henry.demon.co.uk</A> - learned typography at the London College
of Printing, worked on magazine layout in the days before DTP, was part
of the editorial team at Micronet, and marketed BT's Global Network
Services. She is now a freelance Web designer.
<HR>
<A HREF="/~clifeuk/"><IMG ALIGN="MIDDLE" VSPACE="5" HSPACE="5"
SRC="/~clifeuk/graphics/cluklog3.gif" ALT="Computer Life UK
logo"><I>[Back to Computer Life UK Home Page]</I></a>
<HR>
Copyright Ziff-Davis UK Limited 1995. All rights reserved. This
material may not be reproduced or transmitted in any form in whole or
in part without the written consent of the publishers.<P>
<ADDRESS><A
href="mailto:webmaster@ziff.com">webmaster@ziff.com</A></ADDRESS>
</BODY>
</HTML>
```

Figure 7.2 shows the tutorial as rendered by Netscape.

ComputerLife

Create your own home pages

Become at one with the Internet by setting up your own World Wide Web pages. We show you how. *by Anna Smith*

- Step 1 Design a template
- Step 2 Add the words, pictures, and links
- Publish your page
- You want more!?
- Party Tricks
- Don't do this.. at all
- Acronym Alert

Writing your own home pages will give you 15 minutes of fame and stardom - and a healthy respect for the annoying problems that can crop up when you create them. We'll walk you through the basics of how to create a text file that will turn into an HTML file when viewed using a browser such as Netscape.

Ever wondered why some Web pages have those embarrassing line breaks or why not every page is full of graphics? Well, Web pages, written in the text-based browser language known as HTML, can be more than a little tricky to get just right. However, there is a variety of new shareware and commercial packages on the market which make it easier. We've included two software programs on the CD-ROM: HTMLed and Microsoft Word 6.0's Internet Assistant.

Braver souls can write HTML pages using any text editor (including Windows Notepad) and by saving it as a TXT file, just as long as you follow certain basic guidelines. Although the more sophisticated programs automate the process, it's helpful to understand the basics of HTML design when you set out to create your own pages.

Step 1: Design a template

There are certain tags (instructions to a hypertext browser) that you must include in your Web page. It's easiest to put these in first as the bones of your template. To begin, open a file using one of the packages we've included on the CD-ROM or a basic text editor and save the file with an HTM extension. Then add the following text.

<HTML>
The very first tag. This tells the browser that a hypertext page is coming up. If the tag's not there, the browser will display anything that follows as plain text, including all other tags.

<HEAD>
The head of a hypertext page contains information about it: its title and any version/ownership info.

<TITLE>
The title of your page as browsers will see it. The TITLE element always sits between the **<HEAD>** and **</HEAD>** tags and must be plain text only.

</TITLE>
Closes the title part of the page.

Figure 7.2: *ComputerLife's* **Create your own home pages**

EXAMPLE 2—A TUTORIAL PAGE **143**

<!--Your comment here-->
Comment tags. Put the date here, for example. Comments aren't shown on- screen.

</HEAD>
Closes the head part of your page. Now you can go on to the fun bit!

<BODY>
The start tag of the area where you put text, pictures, sound files and pointers to other interesting parts of the Web. Be bold, be smart, be creative! Presentation is crucial, so make your pages a pleasure for others to read.

<HR>
This optional tag displays a horizontal rule across the page. Use it as a visual cue that this is the end of the page. Put your email address under the rule.

</BODY>
Closes the body area.

</HTML>
The very last tag. It closes your hypertext page.

Step 2: Add the words, pictures and links

Headings
It's considered good hypertext practice to make the first element after the opening <BODY> tag a Heading, announcing what your page is about.

There are six levels of Heading, the first of which produces large, bold lettering, with space above and below. Experiment with your HTML editor and various browsers to see what they look like. The tag for a Level One Heading looks like this:-

<H1>

This is a first level heading

</H1>

I've tagged the sentence "This is a first level heading" so you can see what a Level One heading looks like on your browser.

Text
Any text that is not enclosed within tags is shown on-screen as plain text. All HTML documents must be saved as plain ASCII files. Browsers recognise nothing but word-breaks - they won't see the line and paragraph breaks generated by your word processor. You must specify exactly where you want each paragraph to break. Line width changes according to the size of window your reader has chosen on her browser.

Be kind to your readers and keep paragraphs short - a huge block of unbroken text is off-putting.

To break a line, type **
**
The next line starts immediately below.

For a paragraph break, type **<P>**

This inserts a space between the lines.

You may want to emphasise a line or a word. There are two basic attribute tags. The first is:

<STRONG>

Figure 7.2: *ComputerLife's* **Create your own home pages (continued)**

Usually makes your text look bold.
</STRONG>

And the other is:

<EM>
Short for "emphasised". Usually makes your text look italic.
</EM>

Pictures

Pictures should be in GIF or JPEG formats. There are programs available for download which will convert PC graphics into whichever of these two you prefer. JPEGs tend to compress smaller than GIFs (especially with large images), but use a "lossy" algorithm that degrades image quality. Best thing to do is experiment and see how your graphics look in your browser.

The HTML tag for inserting a picture is:

<IMG SRC=yourpic.gif ALT="Picture of a whatever">

Obviously replace **'yourpic.gif'** with the actual name of your graphics file. The ALT tag displays text which describes your picture. It is a courtesy for the benefit of text-only browser users.

Linking to other Web pages

If your home page is all about Star Trek, for example, you'll want to tell other fans where more ST goodies can be found. You do this with what HTML calls an 'anchor' - it's the blue underlined text that you click on to do something or go somewhere. Graphics can be anchors too. This is the tag you use:

<A HREF="http://www.somewhere.co.uk/brilliant_startrek_site.html">
Click here for a brilliant Star Trek site!
</A>

The text between the double quotes is the URL of the Web page you want people to visit. You can also link to FTP sites and newsgroups. Because URLs are case-sensitive, be careful to type them correctly - some use all lower-case letters, some include capital letters. You can also use them to link to additional pages that you create, giving your Home Page more depth.

Publishing Your Page

When you have finished your files, contact your Internet provider for information on how to upload them. It varies from company to company, but many providers are offering free space as part of their sign up offers.

You want more!?

If you want more hints and tips, you can of course find these on the Web itself. Here are a few places to start you off:

The World Wide Web Virtual Library is a cornucopia of links to everything you need to know about making World Wide Web pages. Explore thoroughly!

The Virtual Library's HTML index is where you download The Beginner's Guide to HTML and other info about HTML editing.

Figure 7.2: *ComputerLife's* **Create your own home pages (continued)**

EXAMPLE 3—A SMALL ORGANIZATION'S HOME PAGE   **145**

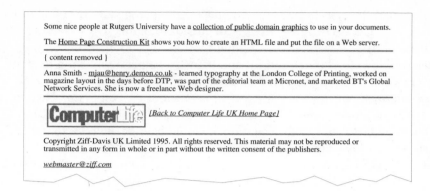

Some nice people at Rutgers University have a <u>collection of public domain graphics</u> to use in your documents.

The <u>Home Page Construction Kit</u> shows you how to create an HTML file and put the file on a Web server.

{ content removed }

Anna Smith - <u>mjau@henry.demon.co.uk</u> - learned typography at the London College of Printing, worked on magazine layout in the days before DTP, was part of the editorial team at Micronet, and marketed BT's Global Network Services. She is now a freelance Web designer.

Computer Life *[Back to Computer Life UK Home Page]*

webmaster@ziff.com

Figure 7.2: *ComputerLife*'s **Create your own home pages (continued)**

EXAMPLE 3—A SMALL ORGANIZATION'S HOME PAGE

The New Jersey Macintosh User's Group (NJMUG) provides this World Wide Web site as a service to its members and the Macintosh user community at large. Most of the page is a collection of links to resources of interest to Macintosh users. The links are organized into a four-row by two-column table, each cell of the table containing an icon and text linked to a subpage in the Webspace. I don't know if it was intentional, but there's not a single heading tag used in the entire document; nevertheless, I feel this is a very nice presentation of information and references. The NJMUG home page was originally developed by Steven Hatch, creative director of The Turnaround Team, Inc. and is now maintained by Jonathan Vafai of Turnaround. The URL of the page is <http://www.intac.com/njmug/njmug.html>.

NJMUG's HTML code starts with a head section containing the page's title and an authorship link as well as some comments to identify the HTML file should it be viewed out of context. The <BODY> tag specifies colors for the background (#015050—a dark cyan), linked text (#FFEE00—a bright yellow) and visited links (#00FFFF—bright cyan). Although the background is fairly dark, it is still light enough that the text can be read on a grayscale display. Immediately following the <BODY> tag is a <CENTER> tag; the corresponding end tag, </CENTER>, is the last item of the HTML source before the closing </BODY> tag. Thus, the entire content of the page is aligned in the center of the reader's display window.

The top of the page begins with an image, njmug_logo.gif, from a subdirectory called images. The image itself is an anchor for a link to a sound file with the URL <http://www.intac.com/njmug/files/njmug.au>. Clicking on the image will download the sound file and launch a helper application to play it. It is a recording of someone reading the welcome message "Welcome to NJ Mug." Following the logo is some text which includes a mail to link back to NJMUG's Webmaster, rendered with citation tags (<CITE></CITE>). Since the enclosed text is not really a citation, it would have been better to use emphasis or italic style tags.

The <IMG> tag pointing to the NJMUG logo uses a bunch of Netscape's attributes. The HEIGHT and WIDTH attributes act to reserve space for the image in order to speed up page formatting. The ALIGN attribute with the value "top," and the HSPACE attributes are not necessary here as the image stands alone. BORDER=0 turns off the frame around the image that would indicate it is an anchor for a link. This is good—the welcome sound clip is a nice touch but not really necessary content and the reader can still determine that there is a link there by the way the mouse pointer changes to a hand when on the image. There's no ALT attribute in the image tag to describe the image for readers who don't automatically load images, but that's okay, too. It's clear from other content that this is the NJMUG home page.

The four-by-two table that is the main part of the page is specified with a two-pixel border which looks very nice. The table tag also specifies four pixels of padding separating the contents of each cell from the cell's walls. Each row of the table is properly enclosed in starting and ending table row tags, <TR></TR>, and, likewise, each data cell is enclosed in starting and ending table data tags, <TD></TD>.

Each data cell in the table is cleverly laid out to consist of an image and strongly emphasized text, both linked to a subpage. The author achieved a nice, clean look by turning off the anchor border that would surround the image. Normally, you would separate images such as these from the following text by inserting a blank between the image tag and the text; in this case, however, that space would have been rendered with an underline since it is part of the anchor. Rather than duplicate the anchor tags for the image and the text, the author has added HSPACE=6 to force the spacing without the underline. Each data cell also specifies VALIGN=middle. This attribute could have been placed in the table rows tags, saving some typing, or, for that matter, eliminated entirely, as it is the default.

```
<HTML>
<HEAD>
```

EXAMPLE 3—A SMALL ORGANIZATION'S HOME PAGE   **147**

```
<!-- OWNER_NAME="Jonathan Vafai" -->
<LINK rev=made href="mailto:jvafai@turnaround.com">
<!-- OWNER_INFO="The Turnaround Team, Inc., Westfield, NJ, 07090-1454" -
->
<TITLE>NJ Macintosh Users Group Web</TITLE>
</HEAD>

<BODY BGCOLOR="#015050" VLINK="#00ffff" link="FFEE00">
<center>
<A HREF="http://www.intac.com/njmug/files/njmug.au">
<IMG  WIDTH=300 HEIGHT=115 SRC="images/njmug_logo.gif" align=top
hspace=6 border=0 ></A>
<p>
<strong>A WWW service of the New Jersey Macintosh Users Group.</strong>
<p>
<cite>Send any feedback to <A
HREF="mailto:webmaster@njmug.org">webmaster@njmug.org</a></cite>
<p>
<table border=2 cellpadding=4>
<TR>
<td valign=middle><A HREF="whats-new.html"><IMG ALIGN=middle WIDTH=46
HEIGHT=42 SRC="images/help.gif" hspace=6 border=0><strong>What's
New?</strong></a></td>
<td valign=middle><A HREF="mug_info.html"><IMG ALIGN=middle WIDTH=46
HEIGHT=42 SRC="images/nj.gif" hspace=6 border=0 ><strong>NJMUG
Info</strong></A></td>
</TR>

<TR>
<td valign=middle><A HREF="njmug_bbs.html"><IMG ALIGN=middle WIDTH=46
HEIGHT=42 SRC="images/phone.gif" hspace=6 border=0 ><strong>NJMUG BBS
Info</strong></A></td>
<td valign=middle><A HREF="commerical.html"><IMG ALIGN=middle WIDTH=46
HEIGHT=42 SRC="images/net.gif" hspace=6 border=0 ><strong>Macintosh Web
Sites</strong></A></td>
</TR>

<TR>
<td valign=middle><A HREF="archives.html"><IMG ALIGN=middle  WIDTH=46
```

```
HEIGHT=42 SRC="images/mac.gif" hspace=6 border=0 ><strong>Macintosh
Software Archives</strong></A></td>
<td valign=middle><A HREF="config.html"><IMG ALIGN=middle WIDTH=46
HEIGHT=42 SRC="images/info.gif" hspace=6 border=0 ><strong>Internet
Configurations</strong></A></td>
</TR>

<TR>
<td valign=middle><A HREF="tools.html"><IMG ALIGN=middle WIDTH=46
HEIGHT=42 SRC="images/files.gif" hspace=6 border=0 ><strong>Macintosh
Internet Tools</strong></A></td>
<td valign=middle><A HREF="usenet.html"><IMG ALIGN=middle WIDTH=46
HEIGHT=42 SRC="images/chat.gif" hspace=6 border=0 ><strong>Macintosh
Newsgroups</strong></A></td>
</TR>
</table>

<br clear>
<p>
<HR>
The number of people who visited the NJMUG Web (recently):
<IMG  WIDTH=56 HEIGHT=16 SRC="http://owl.net/bin/ttt/nj-count.xbm"
align=top hspace=3 ALT="Visit Counter">
<P>
<HR>
<B><FONT SIZE=-2>COPYRIGHT 1995
<A HREF="mailto:webmaster@njmug.org">NJMUG, INC</A>
-- ALL RIGHTS RESERVED
</B></FONT>
</center>
</BODY>
</HTML>
```

After the table, there is a line break tag with the CLEAR attribute and a paragraph break, neither of which is necessary. Following that, between horizontal rules, is a counter of the number of visits to this page. This counter is a service provided by OWL.net, which periodically accesses the usage log of intac.com, counts the number of page hits, and builds the odometer-style image. The page ends with a copyright statement which the author has placed in capital

Example 3—A small organization's home page   **149**

letters. Evidentally this did not look very good to the author, so he tweaked the typography by enclosing the line in font and bold style tags:

```
<B><FONT SIZE=-2> ... </B></FONT>
```

The font tag reduces the size of the text a couple of notches. Note that this works even though the font and bold style tags overlap. Figure 7.3 shows the completed home page.

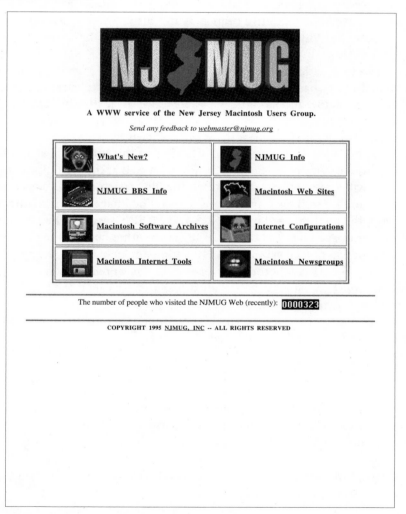

Figure 7.3: NJMUG home page

EXAMPLE 4—A LARGE ORGANIZATION'S HOME PAGE

After showing the previous examples of Web pages of individuals and small organizations, I thought this would be a good place to present an example of the home page of a large organization. On October 20, 1994, Vice President Al Gore announced the availability of The White House World Wide Web Server, an interactive citizens' handbook at <http://www.whitehouse.gov/> . This page, which covers the Executive Branch, is at <http://www.whitehouse.gov/White_House/ EOP/html/3_parts.html>, one jump from the White House home page.

This was a well-designed Web page a year ago. While the Web has gone wild since then, the page has changed imperceptibly. Although still clear and concise, it's a boring page now and has little to elevate it over its text-only alternative at <http://www.whitehouse.gov/White_House/EOP/html/3_parts-plain.html>. For comparison, check out FedWorld at <http://www.fedworld.gov/>.

The page begins with an imagemap. Clicking on this image will send the cursor coordinates to the imagemap program located at the root of the server. Imagemap will look up the coordinates in the file 3_parts.map to determine which URL to link to. This way of doing server-side imagemaps is slightly different from the method used by the NCSA and CERN servers. The page ends with another image map that can take the reader either back to the previous page or to the top of the server. The URL addressing here is also strange and illustrates how HTML can become server-dependent on relatively simple pages. The second imagemap uses a script called *previous*, passing it the URL of the current page as extra path info.

What this page does well is to provide clear options for searching for government information. The link to the FedWorld page

```
<A HREF="/cgi-bin/good-
bye.cgi?url=http://www.fedworld.gov/&current=3_parts.html"> FedWorld</A>
```

is interesting. It calls a CGI script, goodbye.cgi, passing it two arguments: the full URL to link to and the filename of the current page. There is obviously an attempt here to track the progress of readers through this Webspace. Below that is an image of the Capitol. It's referenced with the partial "URL ../images/capitol-icon.gif." The double dots refer to the parent directory of the current page's directory.

What can be done to update this page? My suggestion would be to eleminate the borders around the imagemaps and replace the photographic buttons with icons. The White House, Capitol Building, and the Presidential seal are

EXAMPLE 4—A LARGE ORGANIZATION'S HOME PAGE **151**

such distinctive images (at least to U.S. readers), that simple illustrations would have a more visual impact than the photos used. A nice background for the page could be done by taking the Presidential seal and reducing it to a few shades of very light gray so that it has a watermark effect.

There's a mistake in the HTML code that should be ignored by most browsers. See if you can find an extra ending anchor tag, </A>.

```
<HTML>
<TITLE>Executive Branch</TITLE>
<A HREF="/imagemap/3_parts.map">
<IMG SRC="/White_House/EOP/images/3_parts.gif" ALT="[Clickable Image]"
ISMAP></A>
<P><HR><P>
There are four ways to use this service to look for government
information:
<UL>
<LI>By selecting a government agency from one of the categories in the
image above.
<LI>By agency using
<A HREF="DC_map.html">a map of Washington, D.C.</A>
<LI>By a <A HREF="/cgi-bin/good-
bye.cgi?url=http://www.fedworld.gov/#usgovt&current=3_parts.html">
subject index to government information online</A>, which is provided by
<A HREF="/cgi-bin/good-
bye.cgi?url=http://www.fedworld.gov/&current=3_parts.html">
FedWorld</A>.
<LI>By a <A HREF="http://info.er.usgs.gov/gils/index.html">government
information locator service (GILS)</A>, which is an index being built
to all government information.
</UL>
<P>
<IMG SRC= "../images/capitol-icon.gif" ALT= "[Aerial View of Capitol
Building]"></A>
<A HREF="other_branches.html"> Find Information from Other Branches of
the Government</A>
<P>
<HR>
<A HREF="/White_House/EOP/html/3_parts-plain.html">textual
representation of this page.</A>
<HR>
```

```
<A HREF="/cgi-
bin/previous/0/http://www.whitehouse.gov/White_House/EOP/html/3_parts.ht
ml">
<IMG SRC="/White_House/images/bottom_banner.gif" ALT="[W2WH Footer -
Clickable Image]" ISMAP></A><P>
To comment on this service: <A
HREF="/White_House/Keepers/html/Keepers.html"><I>feedback@www.whitehouse
.gov</I></A>
</HTML>
```

Figure 7.4 shows the Executive Branch page.

Example 5—A page of Internet resources

A Net friend, Larry Chase, first turned me on to the Yahoo catalog when it was still at Stanford University. Yahoo has since become the standard for subject-oriented guides to Internet resources. Three links away from the Yahoo home page is this page at <http://www.rpi.edu/Internet/Guides/decemj/text.html> by John December, entitled Internet Web Text. This page is very good HTML. Unlike some of the other examples in this chapter, I've done very little reformatting to make the code more readable.

Although not reproduced here, this page has one of my favorite background patterns. It's a large grid of very light cyan dots on a white background that gives the effect of the kind of cheap graph paper used in my high school physics courses. The GIF file for this image is not in the same Webspace as this page so it is referenced with a full URL. Other images are referenced with relative addressing.

The page begins with a small transparent gif image followed by a collection of links separated by slashes that provide additional information about the page and alternative versions for nongraphical browsers. The anchors for these links are in italics, aligned with the bottom of the image. Next, following the first horizontal rule is the page title and authorship information. On a resource page such as this, having the last update date at the top is a good move. Note the use of the character entity ç to create Version française.

```
<HTML>
<HEAD>
    <TITLE>Internet Web Text</TITLE>
    <LINK REV=made HREF="mailto:john@december.com">
</HEAD>
<BODY Background="http://www.rpi.edu/~decemj/images/back.gif">
```

EXAMPLE 5—A PAGE OF INTERNET RESOURCES   **153**

Figure 7.4: The White House, Executive Branch page

```
<img src="images/text.gif" ALT="IWT HOME">
<I>
<a href="about.html">README</a> /
<a href="narrative.html">Narrative</a> /
<a href="no-icons.html">No-icons</a> /
<a href="compact.html">Compact version</a> /
<a href="icons.html">Icons-only</a>
</I><BR>
<hr>
<H1>Internet Web Text</H1>
<ADDRESS>
<a href="john_december.html">John December</a> (john@december.com)
</ADDRESS>
<a href="releases.html">Release </a> 1.35; 17 Nov 1995<BR>
<a href="global.html">Global</a> sites:
<a href="http://www.rpi.edu/Internet/Guides/decemj/text.html">New York,
USA</a>
/ Nancy, France
(<a
href="http://www.loria.fr/~charoy/InternetWeb/text.html">English</a>,
<a href="http://www.loria.fr/~charoy/ToileInternet/text.html">Version
fran&ccedil;aise</a>) /
<a href="http://www.unimelb.edu.au/public/decemj/text.html">Melbourne,
Australia</a><BR>
<p>
<hr>
```

The author has added an extra line and paragraph breaks just before the horizontal rule that separates the page's heading from the main text. Browsers are supposed to ignore any extra white space inserted in this manner, but some, including Netscape Navigator, will provide a little bit more. Although it is not considered good HTML to code extra breaks, everybody does it.

After this second horizontal rule begins the main part of the page, beginning with a link to a narrative overview. This entire part of the page is structured as a series of definition lists with <DL></DL> tags enclosing definition term <DT> and definition description <DD> tags. Each definition term (except the first) is composed of two anchors, the first enclosing a small square icon image and the second enclosing a text label. Both point to a single-page version of the information contained in the definition description paired with the definition term. The icon points to a graphic version of the page, the label

EXAMPLE 5—A PAGE OF INTERNET RESOURCES   **155**

to a narrative version. The page ends with a short copyright notice using the character entity © for the copyright symbol (©). Most browsers will now recognize © for this symbol.

```
<DL>
<DT><a href="narrative.html">Narrative Overview</a>
<P>
<DT><a href="orient.html"><img src="images/page.gif" ALT="Orientation
List"></A>
<a href="nar-orient.html">Internet Orientation</A>
<DD>
<a href="ftp://nic.merit.edu/documents/fyi/fyi_20.txt">What is the
Internet? </a>
* <a
href="ftp://nysernet.org/pub/resources/guides/surfing.2.0.3.txt">Surfing
 the Internet</a>
* <a href="ftp://ftp.merit.edu/documents/fyi/fyi_28.txt"> Netiquette</a>
* <a
href="http://pubweb.parc.xerox.com/hypertext/wwwvideo/wwwvideo.html">Xer
ox Overview</A>
* <a href="cyberatlas.html">CyberAtlas</a>
* (<a href="icmc/internet-introduction.html">See also</a>)
</DL>
<DL>
<DT><a href="guides.html"><img src="images/page.gif" ALT="Guides
List"></A>
<a href="nar-guides.html">Guides to Using the Internet</A>
<DD>
<A HREF="http://www.eff.org/papers/eegtti/eegttitop.html">EFF's
Internet Guide</a>  *
<A HREF="http://www.earn.net/gnrt/notice.html#contents">EARN's Guide to
Network Resource Tools</a> *
<A HREF="http://www.eit.com:80/web/www.guide/"> Entering the World-Wide
Web</a>  *
<A HREF="http://sundance.cso.uiuc.edu/Publications/Other/Zen/zen-
1.0_toc.html">Zen and the Art of the Internet</a>  *
<A HREF="http://login.eunet.no/~presno/index.html">The Online
World</a>  *
<A HREF="ftp://uiarchive.cso.uiuc.edu/pub/etext/gutenberg/etext93/
email025.txt">Email 101</a>  *
```

```
<A HREF="http://www.nova.edu/Inter-
Links/UNIXhelp/TOP_.html">UNIXhelp</A>
*
(<a href="http://www.rpi.edu/Internet/Guides/decemj/icmc/internet-
navigating-guides.html">See also</a>)
</DL>
<DL>
<DT><a href="reference.html"><img src="images/page.gif" ALT="Reference
List"></A>
<a href="nar-reference.html">Internet Reference</A>
<DD>
<A HREF="icmc/toc3.html">
Information Sources </a>  *
<A HREF="itools/toc3.html">
Internet Tools</a>  *        <A
HREF="http://www.uwm.edu/Mirror/inet.services.html">
Special Internet Connections</a>  *
<a href="http://www.internic.net">
InterNIC</a>  *
<a href="ftp://nic.merit.edu">
Merit</a>  *
<a href="http://viswiz.gmd.de/MultimediaInfo/">
Multimedia Index</a>  *
<A HREF="ftp://rtfm.mit.edu/pub/usenet/news.answers/internet-
services/faq">
Internet Services FAQ</a>
</DL>
<DL>
<DT><a href="browse.html"><img src="images/page.gif" ALT="Explore
List"></A>
<a href="nar-browse.html">Internet Browsing and Exploring</A>
<DD>
<a href="gopher://gopher.micro.umn.edu:70/1">
Gopher</a>  *
<a href="http://library.usask.ca/hytelnet/">
Hytelnet</a>  *
<a href="http://nearnet.gnn.com/gnn/GNNhome.html">
Global Network Navigator</a>  *
<a href="telnet://library.wustl.edu">
```

EXAMPLE 5—A PAGE OF INTERNET RESOURCES **157**

```
World Window</a>  *
<a href="http://www.hunt.org/">
Internet Hunt</a>  *
<a href="icmc/culture.html">
Cultural Aspects</a>  *
<a href="http://sunsite.unc.edu/expo/ticket_office.html">
World Wide Web Exhibits</a>
</DL>
<DL>
<DT><a href="subject.html"><img src="images/page.gif" ALT="Subjects
List"></A>
<a href="nar-subject.html">Subject-Oriented Searching</A>
<DD>
<a
href="http://www.w3.org/hypertext/DataSources/bySubject/Overview.html">
WWW Virtual Library</a>  *
<a href="http://www.einet.net/galaxy.html">
EINet Galaxy</a>  *
<a href="http://www.yahoo.com/">
ahoo </a>  *
<a href="http://www.lib.umich.edu/chhome.html">
Subject-Oriented Internet Guides</a>  *
<a href="http://galaxy.einet.net/GJ/index.html">
Gopher Jewels</a>  *
<a href="http://www-elc.gnn.com/gnn/wic/wics/index.html">
Whole Internet Catalog</a>  *
<a href="http://www.cis.ohio-state.edu/hypertext/faq/usenet/">
USENET Frequently Asked Questions Archive</a>
*
(<a href="icmc/internet-searching-subjects.html">See also</a>)
</DL>
<DL>
<DT><a href="search.html"><img src="images/page.gif" ALT="Words
List"></A>
<a href="nar-search.html">Word-Oriented Searching</A>
<DD>
<a href="http://cuiwww.unige.ch/meta-index.html">
Web Search</a>
```

```
(<a href="http://cuiwww.unige.ch/w3catalog">Catalog</a>)
/
<a href="http://web.nexor.co.uk/public/cusi/cusi.html">CUSI</a>
/
<a href="http://www_is.cs.utwente.nl:8080/cgi-bin/local/nph-
susil.pl">External info </a>
*
<a href="http://web.nexor.co.uk/mak/doc/robots/robots.html">
WWW Wanderers</a>
(<a href="http://lycos.cs.cmu.edu/">Lycos</a>,
<a href="http://www.town.hall.org/brokers/www-home-
pages/query.html">Harvest</a>,\
<a href="http://webcrawler.com/">Crawler</a>)
*
<a href="http://galaxy.einet.net/gopher/gopher.html">
Gopher Jewels Search</a>  *
<a href="http://www.wais.com/directory-of-servers.html">
WAIS Directory of Servers</a> *
<a href="telnet://info.cnri.reston.va.us:185">
Knowbot</a>  *
<a href="http://www.w3.org/hypertext/DataSources/WWW/Servers.html">
World-Wide Web Servers</a>  *
<a href="http://web.nexor.co.uk/archie.html">ArchiePlexForm</a>
*
(See also: <a href="icmc/internet-searching-keyword.html">keywords</a>,
<a href="icmc/internet-searching-people.html">people</a>)
</DL>
<DL>
<DT><a href="people.html"><img src="images/page.gif" ALT="People
List"></A>
<a href="nar-people.html">Connecting with People</A>
<DD>
<a href="http://www.liszt.com/">
Discussion Lists (LISZT)</a>  *
<a href="gopher://gopher.nd.edu/11/Non-
Notre%20Dame%20Information%20Sources/Phone%20Books--
Other%20Institutions">
Directory Services</a>  *
<a href="http://www.liszt.com/cgi-bin/news.cgi">
```

EXAMPLE 5—A PAGE OF INTERNET RESOURCES **159**

```
Usenet Newsgroups</a>  *
<a href="http://www.kei.com/irc.html">
Internet Relay Chat</a>  *
<a href="http://www.cis.upenn.edu/~lwl/mudinfo.html">
Multiple User Dialogues</a> *
<a href="icmc/culture-people-lists.html">
People Lists (directories, home pages)</a> *
(<a href="itools/cmc.html">See also: CMC Forums</a>)
</DL>
<hr>
<A HREF="http://www.rpi.edu/Internet/Guides/decemj/icmc/toc3.html"><img
src="http://www.rpi.edu/Internet/Guides/decemj/images/icmc.gif"
ALT="CMC "></A>
<A
HREF="http://www.rpi.edu/Internet/Guides/decemj/itools/toc3.html"><img
src="http://www.rpi.edu/Internet/Guides/decemj/images/itools.gif"
ALT="TOOLS "></A>
<A Href="http://www.rpi.edu/~decemj/cmc/center.html"><IMG
Src="http://www.rpi.edu/~decemj/cmc/images/icon.gif" ALT="CMC
StudieS"></A>
<A Href="http://www.rpi.edu/~decemj/works/wwwu.html"><IMG
Src="http://www.rpi.edu/~decemj/works/wwwu/images/icon.gif" ALT="WWW
Unleashed"></A>
<I>
<A HREF="copyright.html">Copyright &#169 1994, 1995</A> by
<a href="http://www.rpi.edu/~decemj/index.html">John December</a> (<a
href="mailto:decemj@rpi.edu">decemj@rpi.edu</a> )
</I>
</BODY>
</HTML>
```

Figure 7.5 shows how the Internet Web Text page generated by this HTML code will appear when displayed and printed using Netscape Navigator.

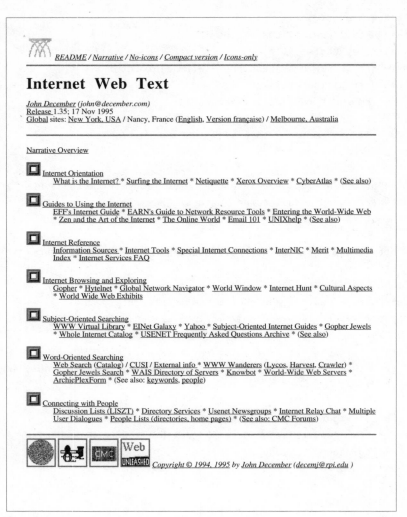

Figure 7.5: A page listing Internet resources

Example 6—A page covering a subject field **161**

Example 6—A page covering a subject field

This is one of my favorite pages on the Web. I met Dr. Godwin-Jones at the Second International World Wide Web Conference, where his Web work was presented in a poster session. I love languages, both natural and artificial, and this page is rich in resources. Dr. Godwin-Jones has made excellent use of a design metaphor. He has equated a visit to his Webspace with the experience of a well organized camping trip. It works. The Trail Guide is a compact backpack of information, with everything clearly labeled and accessible. The page is accessible from the Virgina Commonwealth University's home page at: <http://www.vcu.edu/>161161.

The HTML code begins with a body tag specifying page colors: white for the background, medium red for the text, medium green for both new and visited links. The image at the top of the page has similiar colors; a nice effect of earth and forest colors complementing the Trail Guide metaphor. Below the image is a block of links to other Web servers at Virginia Commonwealth University, and shortcuts—internal links to headings further on in the page. The author has taken a chance here, using the character string "-->" as an arrow, sort of an ASCII graphic. This string is the ending sequence for comments and it's possible that some browsers will incorrectly interpret the code. If there are other HTML errors in the file, this only makes it worse. Netscape is good at handling these fine points of character recognition; other browsers are not. As a rule, always use > for the greater than sign.

The remainder of the page is a series of sections. Starting with Scenic Side Trails, each section is introduced with a level 3 heading containing an image with a transparent background and heading text. At the end of each section is a return button that takes the reader back to the top of the page. The return button is aligned to the right margin, but no text is allowed to wrap around it. Here's how it does it:

```
<a href = #top><img src =
http://www.vcu.edu/hasweb/for/gifs/backarrow.gif align=right></a><br
clear=all>
```

Overall, the page achieves a good balance between compactness and accessibility but does so by breaking a few rules and, while it may not look great in some low-end browsers, it will still do what it's supposed to do—provide a clear and compact guide to Internet resources on a single subject.

```
<html>
<head>
<TITLE> International Guide</TITLE>
</head>
<body bgcolor = "#FFFFFF" TEXT="#7f0000" LINK="#5C4033" VLINK="#5C4033">
<img  src = "http://www.vcu.edu/hasweb/for/gifs/trail.gif"
alt= "VCU INTERNATIONAL TRAIL GUIDE"><BR>
<b> <i> <a name = top>Foreign Language</a> --> </i> </b>
<A HREF="dept/dept.html">Dept</A> /  <a
href=faculty/faculty.html>Faculty</a>  / <a
href=courses/coursepage.html>Courses</a> / <A
HREF="lab/lab.html">Lab</A>    <b><i>Trails --> </i> </b> <A
HREF=traillog/traillog.html> New</a> / <A
HREF=traillog/trail.html>Add</A> <br>
<b><i>Shortcuts  --> </i> </b> <a href=#French>French</a> - <a
href=#German>German</a> - <a href=#Italian>Italian</a> - <a
href=#Russian>Russian</a> - <a href=#Spanish>Spanish</a> - <a
href=#General>General</a><br>
<b><i>Teaching  --> </i> </b>  <a href = #Resources>Links</a> - <a href
= "cgi/interact.html">Language Interactive</a>  - <a href =
"ld/ld.html">Instant Access Treasure Chest</a>
<H3><img align=bottom src =
"http://www.vcu.edu/hasweb/for/gifs/hiker.gif">
Scenic Side Trails</H3>
<A HREF="http://mistral.enst.fr/">WebMuseum</A>  (English) Ever-
expanding gallery of art &  music, plus tour of Paris<br>
<a href = "http://mistral.enst.fr/gn/>Les Guignols de l'Info</a>
(French) Greatest force in French politics in audio & video<br>
<a href =
"http://www.netville.de/artware/projects/verhuellung.html">Wrapped
Reichstag</a> (German) Christo's lastest project in word and deed<br>
<A HREF= "ftp://kiwi.cs.berkeley.edu/pub/music/cuban-music.html">Cuban
Music</A>  (English/Spanish) Listen to sound samples from the forbidden
Isle
<H3>
<IMG ALIGN=bottom SRC="http://www.vcu.edu/hasweb/for/gifs/compass.gif">
Explore by Map</H3>
```

Example 6—A page covering a subject field   **163**

```
<UL>
<LI> <A HREF="http://wings.buffalo.edu/world/">Worldwide WWW sites</A>
(Virtual Tourist -- country by country list of servers)
<LI> <a HREF = "http://wings.buffalo.edu/world/vt2/">Country and City
Guides</a> (CityNet -- pointers to many other resources)
</UL>
<a href = #top><img src =
http://www.vcu.edu/hasweb/for/gifs/backarrow.gif align=right></a><br
clear=all>
<H3><IMG SRC="http://www.vcu.edu/hasweb/for/gifs/tent.gif">
Where to Pitch Your Tent: Recommended Sites</H3><dl><dl><b>
<a name=General>General Collections</a></b> [See also <a href =
"#Resources">Other Resources</a>]</dl></dl>
<a href =
"http://www.willamette.edu/~tjones/languages/WWW_Virtual_Library_Languag
e.html">Human-Languages Page</a> Extensive list  (WWW Virtual Library
site)<br>
 <a href =
"http://www.itp.berkeley.edu/~thorne/HumanResources.html">Foreign
Language Resources on the Web</a> A well-selected list from Berkeley<br>
<a href = "http://grafton.dartmouth.edu:8001/lrc/">Dartmouth Language
Resource Center</a> Links to many Dartmouth & other resources<br>
<a href = "http://babel.uoregon.edu/Yamada.html">Yamada Language
Center</a> Especially valuable for downloadable font collections<p>
<dl><dl><b><a name = "Asian_Studies">Asian Studies</a></b> [See also <a
href = #Chinese>Chinese Lang/Lit</a>]</dl></dl>
<A HREF= "http://coombs.anu.edu.au/WWWVL-AsianStudies.html">Asian
Studies</A> An extensive list (WWW virtual library site)<p>
<dl><dl><b><a name = "French_Studies">French Studies</a></b> [See also
<a href = #French>French Lang/Lit</a> & <A href = "#Camp_Circle">Sound
& Light</a>]</dl></dl>
<a href = "http://www.utm.edu/departments/french/french.html>Famous
French Links</a> Extensive list by the indefatigable "Tennessee Bob"<br>
<A HREF= "http://cuisg13.unige.ch:8100/franco.html">Le coin des
francophones et autres grenouilles</A> Info on a variety of things
French<br>
<a href =
http://freenet.vcu.edu/education/cvanetgv/gvfrench.html>Global Village
French Quarter</a> Extensive list from the U. of Richmond<br>
```

```
<a href = "wif/foyerwif.html>Le Foyer WIF</a> Women in French Page by
Kathryn Murphy-Judy of VCU<p>
<dl><dl><b><a name = "German_Studies">German Studies</a></b> [See also
<a href = #German>German Lang/Lit</a> & <A href = "#Camp_Circle">Sound
& Light</a>]</dl></dl>
<a href = "http://www.rz.uni-
karlsruhe.de/Outerspace/VirtualLibrary/">German Subject Catalog</a>
Good starting point (WWW virtual library site) <br>
<a href = "http://www.uncg.edu/~lixlpurc/german.html">German Studies
Trails</a> Well-maintained list by Andreas Lixl-Purcell<br>
<a href = "http://www.reed.edu/~ccampbel/tkp/links.html">The Kassandra
Project: externities</a> Nicely annotated resource list<p>
<dl><dl><b><a name = "Italian_Studies">Italian Studies</a></b> [See
also <a href = #Italian>Italian Lang/Lit</a>]</dl></dl>
<a href = "http://www.mi.cnr.it:80/IGST/>Italian General Subject
Tree</a> Very comprehensive list (WWW virtual library site)<p>
<dl><dl><b><a name = Latin_American_Studies>Latin American/Spanish
Studies</a></b> [See also <a href = #Spanish>Spanish
Lang/Lit</a>]</dl></dl>
<A HREF="http://lanic.utexas.edu/las.html">Latin American Studies</A>
Indices to 11 countries<br>
<A HREF="http://lanic.utexas.edu>Latin American Network Information
Center</a> Comprehensive site from U. Texas<br>
<a href = "pagina/title.html>La P&aacute;gina Espa&ntilde;ola</a>
Country by country list collected by Andr&eacute; Thomas of VCU<p>
<dl><dl><b>Medieval Studies</b></dl></dl>
<A HREF= "http://www.georgetown.edu/labyrinth/labyrinth-
home.html">Labyrinth</A> Outstanding site and links, Georgetown
University<br>
<a href = "/mdf/mdf.html">International Marie de France Society</a>
Pages by Chantal Mar&eacute;chal of VCU<p>
<dl><dl><b><a name = Russian_Studies>Russian/East European
Studies</a></b> [See also <a href = #Russian>Russian
Lang/Lit</a>]</dl></dl>
<A HREF= "http://www.pitt.edu/~cjp/rees.html">Russian and East
European  Studies</A> Excellent; info on Russian Web servers<br>
<A HREF="http://www2.uncg.edu/~lixlpurc/russian.html">On-line Russian
Studies</a> Good starting place for Russian studies on the Internet<br>
<a href="rus/homepage.html">VCU Russian Page</a>
```

Example 6—A page covering a subject field **165**

```
<a href = #top><img src =
http://www.vcu.edu/hasweb/for/gifs/backarrow.gif align=right></a><br
clear=all>
<H3><IMG ALIGN=bottom
SRC="http://www.vcu.edu/hasweb/for/gifs/campfire.gif" >
Campfire Reading: Language Resources and Texts</H3>
[For languages not taught at VCU, consult the <a href =
"http://www.willamette.edu/~tjones/languages/WWW_Virtual_Library_Languag
e.html">Human-Languages Page</a>] <p>
<b><a name=Chinese>CHINESE Language/Literature</a></b> [See also <a
href = #Asian_Studies>Asian Studies</a>]
<UL>
<LI> <A HREF= "http://nearnet.gnn.com/wic/lit.15.html">Chinese
Literature</A> (novels, poetry and classics; FTP)
<LI> <A HREF= "http://www.c3.lanl.gov/~cim/chinese.html">Chinese
language-related info</A> (excellent guide)
</UL>
<b><a name=French>FRENCH Language/Literature</a></b> [See also <a href
= #French_Studies>French Studies</a>]
<UL>
<LI> <a HREF = "http://www-resus.univ-
mrs.fr/Us/France/grammaire.html">Testez votre grammaire</a> Form-based
grammar quiz
<LI> <A HREF = "http://town.hall.org/travel/france/rfi.html">Parler au
Quotidien</a> Learn French through this popular radio program
<LI> <A HREF= "http://tuna.uchicago.edu/images/heures/heures.html"> Les
tr&egrave;s riches heures du duc du Berry</A> (includes images)
<LI> <A HREF= "http://www.lib.virginia.edu/etext/french.html">French
texts</A> (from U.of Virginia:  from medieval to modern; information)
<LI> <A HREF= "http://tuna.uchicago.edu:/ARTFL.html">French Literature
Collection</A> (ARTFL Project at the U.of Chicago)
<LI> <A HREF="http://philae.sas.upenn.edu/French/french.html">UPenn
resources on the crusades</a>
<ul>
<LI> <A HREF=traillog/frenchlog.html>Hikers' Picks</a> (Sites suggested
by users of this <b>Trail Guide</b>)
<LI> <a href=courses/coursepage.html#Frenchcourses>VCU French
classes</a> (Course home pages)
</ul>
```

```
</UL>
<b><a name=German>GERMAN</a> Language/Literature</b> [See also <a href
= #German_Studies>German Studies</a>]
<UL>
<LI> <A HREF="http://www.fmi.uni-passau.de/htbin/lt/ltd">German-
English</A>  or <A HREF="http://www.fmi.uni-
passau.de/htbin/lt/lte">English-German</A> Dictionary (interactive)
<LI> <A HREF=
"gopher://alpha.epas.utoronto.ca/11/cch/disciplines/german">German
Language Resources</A> (gopher)
<LI> <A HREF= "menu.html">19th-Century Stories</A> (Struwwelpeter,
Busch, Grimm Bros. from VCU)
<LI> <A
HREF="gopher://gopher.epas.utoronto.ca/11/cch/disciplines/german/texts/i
ds">German Literature searchable corpus</A> (Goethe, Thomas Mann, Marx;
telnet)
<LI> <A HREF="http://www.nda.net/nda/spiegel">Access to <b>Der
Spiegel</b> magazine</a> (selected articles only)
<LI> <A HREF="http://www.rz.uni-karlsruhe.de/misc/germnews/">German
news summaries</a>
<ul>
<LI> <A HREF=traillog/germanlog.html>Hikers' Picks</a> (Sites suggested
by users of this <b>Trail Guide</b>)
<LI> <a href=courses/coursepage.html#Germancourses>VCU German
classes</a> (Course home pages)</ul>
</UL>
<b><a name=Italian>ITALIAN Language/Literature</a></b> [See also <a
href = #Italian_Studies>Italian Studies</a>]
<UL>
<LI> <A HREF=
"http://insti.physics.sunysb.edu/~mmartin/languages/italian/italian.html
">Italian for Travellers</a> Basic phrases, links to other resources
<LI> <A HREF= "http://www.crs4.it/HTML/Literature.html">Italian
literature</A> (from Divine Comedy (selections) to Pinocchio; hypertext)
<LI> <A HREF= "gopher://gopher.dartmouth.edu/1/AnonFTP/pub/Dante">Dante
roject</A> (collects 600 years of Dante commentary; gopher)
 <LI> <A HREF= "http://www.crs4.it/~ruggiero/unione.html">"L'Unione
Sarda" on-line</A> (Italian; hypertext)
<LI> <A HREF="gopher://italia.hum.utah.edu:70/1">Italian Language
```

EXAMPLE 6—A PAGE COVERING A SUBJECT FIELD **167**

```
Resources Gopher</a>
<ul>
<LI> <A HREF=traillog/italianlog.html>Hikers' Picks</a> (Sites
suggested by users of this <b>Trail Guide</b>)</ul>
</UL>
<b>LATIN Language & Literature</b>
<UL>
<LI> <A
HREF="gopher://wiretap.spies.com/00/Library/Article/Language/latin.stu"
TITLE=Study>Study Guide to Wheelock Latin</A> (text)
</UL>
<b><a name=Russian>RUSSIAN Language/Literature</a></b> [See also <a
href = #Russian_Studies>Russian/East European Studies</a>]
<UL>
<LI> <A
HREF="http://sunsite.oit.unc.edu/sergei/Grandsons.html">Dazhdbog's
Grandsons</A>  (info on how to handle cyrillic on the Internet)
<LI> <A HREF="http://solar.rtd.utk.edu/friends/home.html">Friends and
Parners</A> (more on cyrillic on the Internet)
<LI> <A HREF="gopher://english-
server.hss.cmu.edu/11ftp%3aEnglish%20Server%3aLanguage%3aRussian%3a"
TITLE=Russian>Russian</A> (gopher)
<ul>
<LI> <A HREF=traillog/russianlog.html>Hikers' Picks</a> (Sites
suggested by users of this <b>Trail Guide</b>)</ul>
</UL>
<b><a name=Spanish>SPANISH Language/Literature</a></b> [See also <a
href = #Latin_American_Studies>Latin American/Spanish Studies</a>]
<UL>
<LI> <A HREF="http://sunsite.unc.edu/expo/1492.exhibit/Intro.html">1492
materials</a> (Exhibit from the Library of Congress)
<LI> <A HREF="http://www.uco.es/cordoba/prologo.html">La cuidad de
Cordoba</a>
<LI> <A HREF="http://www.udg.mx/cultfolk/mexico.html">Mexico, Arte y
Cultura</a>
<ul>
<LI> <A HREF=traillog/spanishlog.html>Hikers' Picks</a> (Sites
suggested by users of this <b>Trail Guide</b>)
<LI> <a href=courses/coursepage.html#Spanishcourses>VCU Spanish
```

```
classes</a> (Course home pages)</ul>
</ul>
<a href = #top><img src =
http://www.vcu.edu/hasweb/for/gifs/backarrow.gif align=right></a><br
clear=all>
<H3><a name = Camp_Circle><IMG ALIGN=bottom
SRC="http://www.vcu.edu/hasweb/for/gifs/moon2.gif">Camp Circle:  Sound
& Light Shows</a></h3>
<dl><dl><dl><b>Multimedia</b></dl></dl></dl>
<A HREF= "http://www.paris.org/parisF.html>The Paris Pages</a> A very
nicely done multimedia tour<br>
 <A HREF="http://www.culture.fr/culture/gvpda.htm">French cave
drawings</A>  Stunning pictures of the recently discovered caves<br>
<a HREF = "huckebein/hans.html">Hans Huckebein</a> Multimedia version
of Wilhelm Busch's story
</dl><p>
<dl><dl><dl><b>Broadcasters</b></dl></dl></dl>
<a href = "http://fbwww.epfl.ch/french/">Fr&eacute;quence Banane</a>
Swiss student radio station (audio files)<br>
<a href = "http://www.tv5.ca/">TV5</a> International French
television<p>
<a href = "http://www.dmc.net/">Deutsche Welle</a> Real-time daily news
broadcasts in German<br>
<A HREF="http://www-dw.gmd.de/deutsch/index/html">Deutsche Welle</a>
Schedules and information (German television)<p>
<A HREF =
"gopher://bluejay.creighton.edu/11/aux/scola/schedule">SCOLA</A>
Schedule of satellite foreign language broadcasts<br>
<A href = "gopher://gopher.VOA.GOV:70/11/audio">Voice of America
broadcasts</a> Not available from many US sites
<a href = #top><img src =
http://www.vcu.edu/hasweb/for/gifs/backarrow.gif align=right></a><br
clear=all>
<H3><IMG ALIGN=bottom
SRC="http://www.vcu.edu/hasweb/for/gifs/globei.gif">
<a name=Resources>Other Language Learning  & Teaching Resources</a>
</H3>
<UL>
<b>External Links</b><br>
```

Example 6—A page covering a subject field **169**

```
<LI> <a href =
"http://polyglot.lss.wisc.edu/lss/lang/teach.html">Teaching with the
Web</a> by Lauren Rosen/UW-Madison
<LI> Review of <A HREF =
http://ubvm.cc.buffalo.edu:80/~listserv/FLTEACH/flteach.fllists>Internet
/Bitnet discussion groups</A> for language learning
<LI> Information about <a
href=http://www.itp.berkeley.edu/~thorne/MOO.html>MOO's</a> in foreign
languages
<LI> <A
HREF="http://www.cortland.edu/www_root/flteach/flteach.html">FLTeach</a>
 home page of the internet discussion group
<li> <a href = "http://www.stolaf.edu/network/iecc">
Intercultural E-mail classroom project</a> - if you're interested in
having your students correspond via e-mail with other students.<p>
<b>VCU Guides</b><br>
<LI> <a href= "ld/ld.html">Instant Access Treasure Chest</a> Learning
Disabilities and Language Learning
<LI> <a href = "cgi/interact.html">Language Interactive</a> Web Forms
and CGI Scripts for Language Learning
<LI> Web <a href = "www.html">Basics</a> -- Demos of using the <a
href=samples/forms.html>WWW for language learning</a>
</UL>
<a href = #top><img src =
http://www.vcu.edu/hasweb/for/gifs/backarrow.gif align=right></a><br
clear=all>
<hr>
<a href=http://www.vcu.edu>VCU</a> -
<A HREF="dept/dept.html">Foreign Language Department</A> - <a
href=courses/coursepage>Courses</a> -
<A HREF=traillog/trailmenu.html>New Trails</a> - <A
HREF=traillog/trail.html>Add a trail</A> - <a
href=traillog/funlog.html>Fun stuff</a> <BR>
<font size = -1>This page does <b>not</b> aim for completeness; sites
are selected based on languages taught at VCU.</font>
<HR>
Copyright 1994  Robert Godwin-Jones
<address>rgjones@cabell.vcu.edu: <a href=faculty/gj.html>home page</a>
/ <a href=mail/mail-gj.html>e-mail</a> / <a href=serverinfo.html>server
```

```
info</a>
</address><br>
Last update:  7/6/95<br> (This site maintained with the active
assistance of <a href=/faculty/sm.html>Sonja Moore</a>)
</body>
</html>
```

One problem with this HTML code is the inconsistent use of double quote marks around URLs. Figure 7.6 shows the VCU Trail Guide page generated by this HTML code as it appears when displayed and printed using Netscape Navigator version 1.12. Version 2.0 of Netscape is not as tolerant of unbalanced quotes and actually loses a few lines of the page. Hopefully the author will have cleaned up these problems by the time you read this.

EXAMPLE 6—A PAGE COVERING A SUBJECT FIELD   **171**

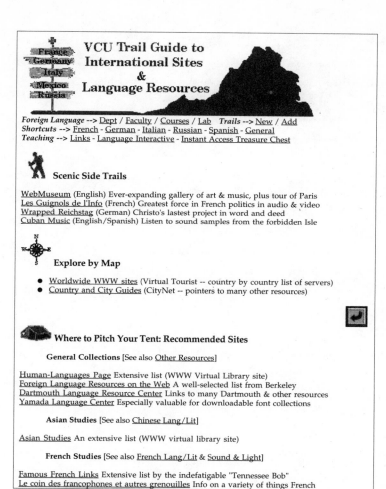

Figure 7.6: VCU Trail Guide to International Sites & Language Resources

Global Village French Quarter Extensive list from the U. of Richmond
Le Foyer WIF Women in French Page by Kathryn Murphy-Judy of VCU

German Studies [See also German Lang/Lit & Sound & Light]

German Subject Catalog Good starting point (WWW virtual library site)
German Studies Trails Well-maintained list by Andreas Lixl-Purcell
The Kassandra Project: externities Nicely annotated resource list

Italian Studies [See also Italian Lang/Lit]

Italian General Subject Tree Very comprehensive list (WWW virtual library site)

Latin American/Spanish Studies [See also Spanish Lang/Lit]

Latin American Studies Indices to 11 countries
Latin American Network Information Center Comprehensive site from U. Texas
La Página Española Country by country list collected by André Thomas of VCU

Medieval Studies

Labyrinth Outstanding site and links, Georgetown University
International Marie de France Society Pages by Chantal Maréchal of VCU

Russian/East European Studies [See also Russian Lang/Lit]

Russian and East European Studies Excellent; info on Russian Web servers
On-line Russian Studies Good starting place for Russian studies on the Internet
VCU Russian Page

 Campfire Reading: Language Resources and Texts

[For languages not taught at VCU, consult the Human-Languages Page]

CHINESE Language/Literature [See also Asian Studies]

- Chinese Literature (novels, poetry and classics; FTP)
- Chinese language-related info (excellent guide)

FRENCH Language/Literature [See also French Studies]

- Testez votre grammaire Form-based grammar quiz
- Parler au Quotidien Learn French through this popular radio program
- Les très riches heures du duc du Berry (includes images)
- French texts (from U.of Virginia: from medieval to modern; information)
- French Literature Collection (ARTFL Project at the U.of Chicago)

Figure 7.6: VCU Trail Guide to International Sites & Language Resources (continued)

EXAMPLE 6—A PAGE COVERING A SUBJECT FIELD **173**

- UPenn resources on the crusades
  - ○ Hikers' Picks (Sites suggested by users of this **Trail Guide**)
  - ○ VCU French classes (Course home pages)

GERMAN Language/Literature [See also German Studies]

- German-English or English-German Dictionary (interactive)
- German Language Resources (gopher)
- 19th-Century Stories (Struwwelpeter, Busch, Grimm Bros. from VCU)
- German Literature searchable corpus (Goethe, Thomas Mann, Marx; telnet)
- Access to **Der Spiegel** magazine (selected articles only)
- German news summaries
  - ○ Hikers' Picks (Sites suggested by users of this **Trail Guide**)
  - ○ VCU German classes (Course home pages)

ITALIAN Language/Literature [See also Italian Studies]

- Italian for Travellers Basic phrases, links to other resources
- Italian literature (from Divine Comedy (selections) to Pinocchio; hypertext)
- Dante Project (collects 600 years of Dante commentary; gopher)
- "L'Unione Sarda" on-line (Italian; hypertext)
- Italian Language Resources Gopher
  - ○ Hikers' Picks (Sites suggested by users of this **Trail Guide**)

LATIN Language & Literature

- Study Guide to Wheelock Latin (text)

RUSSIAN Language/Literature [See also Russian/East European Studies]

- Dazhdbog's Grandsons (info on how to handle cyrillic on the Internet)
- Friends and Parners (more on cyrillic on the Internet)
- Russian (gopher)
  - ○ Hikers' Picks (Sites suggested by users of this **Trail Guide**)

SPANISH Language/Literature [See also Latin American/Spanish Studies]

- 1492 materials (Exhibit from the Library of Congress)
- La cuidad de Cordoba
- Mexico, Arte y Cultura
  - ○ Hikers' Picks (Sites suggested by users of this **Trail Guide**)
  - ○ VCU Spanish classes (Course home pages)

 Camp Circle: Sound & Light Shows

Figure 7.6: VCU Trail Guide to International Sites & Language Resources (continued)

Multimedia

The Paris Pages A very nicely done multimedia tour
French cave drawings Stunning pictures of the recently discovered caves
Hans Huckebein Multimedia version of Wilhelm Busch's story

Broadcasters

Fréquence Banane Swiss student radio station (audio files)
TV5 International French television

Deutsche Welle Real-time daily news broadcasts in German
Deutsche Welle Schedules and information (German television)

SCOLA Schedule of satellite foreign language broadcasts
Voice of America broadcasts Not available from many US sites

Other Language Learning & Teaching Resources

External Links
- Teaching with the Web by Lauren Rosen/UW-Madison
- Review of Internet/Bitnet discussion groups for language learning
- Information about MOO's in foreign languages
- FLTeach home page of the internet discussion group
- Intercultural E-mail classroom project - if you're interested in having your students correspond via e-mail with other students.

VCU Guides
- Instant Access Treasure Chest Learning Disabilities and Language Learning
- Language Interactive Web Forms and CGI Scripts for Language Learning
- Web Basics -- Demos of using the WWW for language learning

VCU - Foreign Language Department - Courses - New Trails - Add a trail - Fun stuff
This page does **not** aim for completeness; sites are selected based on languages taught at VCU.

Copyright 1994 Robert Godwin-Jones
rgjones@cabell.vcu.edu: *home page* / *e-mail* / *server info*

Last update: 7/6/95
(This site maintained with the active assistance of Sonja Moore)

Figure 7.6: VCU Trail Guide to International Sites & Language Resources (continued)

Appendix A:
HTML Quick Reference

The following listing of HTML markup elements is taken from the HTML 2.0 specification, the draft HTML 3.0 specification, and the release notes from Netscape Navigator. It should be considered neither definitive nor 100 percent complete, but, rather, a compact guide to the most useful and commonly found features of Hypertext Markup Language.

The presentation of each markup element includes the syntax of the tag, a short description, and the attributes that can be specified with the tag. The syntax description takes one of two forms, for example:

<IMG>   Indicates an empty tag

<H1>...</H1>   Indicates a container or nonempty tag. The ellipsis (...) stands for some portion (possibly none) of the document's content.

Attributes take one of two forms: Either attribute="value", where value is some text enclosed in quotes, or just simply attribute without a value. In the table below, value may take one of the following forms:

url	The value is a Uniform Resource Locator.
name	The value is a name supplied by the user.
number	The value is a number supplied by the user.
percent	The value is a percentage (number%).
pixels	The value is a whole number of pixels.

nchars	The value is a whole number of character positions.
text	The value is a text supplied by the user.
color	The value is an rgb color value (#rrggbb).
server	The value is server-dependent text.
x,y	The value is a coordinate measured in pixels.
[A	B	...]	The value is one from a fixed set of values, A, B, ...

COMMON ATTRIBUTES

Attribute	Definition
ALIGN	Specifies the alignment of content with respect to the reader's display window. Possible values are: "left", "center", "right", and "justify".
CLASS	Provides a name token that classifies the element and can be addressed in style sheets. The value is an SGML name.
ID	Provides a name for the location of the element on the page that can be referenced by anchors and other HTML elements. The value is an SGML name.
LANG	Designates the language conventions to be used with respect to quotation marks, ligatures, and scan direction.

STYLE MARKUP

Style markup is permitted within all other HTML markup. Structural markup should be avoided within style markup. In the following descriptions of HTML markup a code is used to indicate the source: (N) means the feature is a Netscape extension, (3) means the feature is from HTML 3.0 draft specification, and (D) means the feature is depreciated and has fallen from general use. Otherwise, the feature is from the HTML 2.0 specification.

Tag	Description	Attributes
<ABBREV>... </ABBREV>	Abbreviation (3)	
<ACRONYM>... </ACRONYM>	Acronym style (3)	

Tag	Description	Attributes
<B>...</B>	Bold style	
<BIG>...</BIG>	Big style. Display text using a larger font (3)	
<BLINK>...</BLINK>	Blinking text (N)	
<CITE>...</CITE>	Citation style. For titles of other works	
<CODE>...</CODE>	Coding style. For samples of computer programs	
<DEL>...</DEL>	For marking deleted text as in legal documents (3)	
<DFN>...</DFN>	The defining instance of a term (3)	
<EM>...</EM>	Emphasis	
<FONT>...</FONT>	Specifies font attributes (N)	SIZE=±number COLOR=color
<I>...</I>	Italics style	
<INS>...</INS>	For marking inserted text as in legal documents (3)	
<KBD>...</KBD>	Keyboard style for text to be keyed exactly as given (D)	
<PERSON>...</PERSON>	Marks names of people to allow them to be highlighted or extracted by indexing programs (3)	
<Q>...</Q>	Quoted text. Show in quotation marks appropriate to the language context (3)	
<SAMP>...</SAMP>	Sample style. Used for examples (D)	
<SMALL>...</SMALL>	Small style. Display text using a smaller font (3)	

Tag	Description	Attributes
<STRIKE>...</STRIKE>	Strikethrough style	
<STRONG>...</STRONG>	Strong emphasis style	
_{...}	Subscript (N,3)	
^{...}	Superscript (N,3)	
<TT>...</TT>	Typewriter style	
<VAR>...</VAR>	Variable style. For names to be supplied by reader (D)	

STRUCTURAL MARKUP

With only a few exceptions, structural markup inside of other stuctural markup should be avoided. The exceptions are the <CENTER>, <DIV>, <DD>, <DT>, <FIGURE> <FORM>, <TH>, and <TD> tags, which can be used within any other markup.

BLOCK ELEMENTS

Tag	Description	Attributes
<ADDRESS>...</ADDRESS>	Address style. Used for addresses, signatures, authorship info, and so on	
<BLOCKQUOTE>...</BLOCKQUOTE>	For material quoted from an external source	
 	Line break. Starts a new line	
<CENTER>...</CENTER>	Center page content (N)	
<DIV>...</DIV>	Division. For classifying a subsection of the document (N,3)	
<FN>...</FN>	Footnote (3)	

Tag	Description	Attributes
<H1>...</H1>	Level 1 heading	
<H2>...</H2>	Level 2 heading	
<H3>...</H3>	Level 3 heading	
<H4>...</H4>	Level 4 heading	
<H5>...</H5>	Level 5 heading	
<H6>...</H6>	Level 6 heading	
<HR>	Horizontal rule. Draws a line across the page	SIZE=pixels WIDTH=percent NOSHADE
<NOTE>...</NOTE>	An auxiliary paragraph (3)	ROLE=name
<PRE>...</PRE>	Preformatted style	WIDTH=nchars
<P>...</P>	Paragraph break	
<TAB>	Horizontal tab (3)	TO=name INDENT=nchars

LIST ELEMENTS

Tag	Description	Attributes
<DIR>...</DIR>	Directory list. Used for lists typically containing short items such as file names. Uses <LI> (D)	
<DL>...</DL>	Definition list. Used for glossaries. Uses <DT> and <DD>	
<DD>...</DD>	Definition description, part of a definition list item	
<DT>...</DT>	Definition term, part of a definition list item	
<LI>...</LI>	List item	
<MENU>...</MENU>	Menu list. Uses <LI> (D)	
<OL>...</OL>	Ordered list. Uses <LI>	
<UL>...</UL>	Unordered list. Uses <LI>	COMPACT

TABLE ELEMENTS

Tag	Description	Attributes
<TABLE>...</TABLE>	Defines a table	BORDER=pixels WIDTH=percent CELLSPACING=pixels CELLPADDING=pixels
<CAPTION>...</CAPTION>	Defines a caption to a table	ALIGN=[TOP | BOTTOM]
<TR>...</TR>	Table row	ALIGN=[LEFT | CENTER | RIGHT] VALIGN=[TOP | MIDDLE | BOTTOM]
<TD>...</TD>	Table Data cell	ROWSPAN=number COLSPAN=number ALIGN=[LEFT | CENTER | RIGHT] VALIGN=[TOP | MIDDLE | BOTTOM]
<TH>...</TH>	Table Header cell. Contents bold and centered	ROWSPAN=number COLSPAN=number ALIGN=[LEFT | CENTER | RIGHT] VALIGN=[TOP | MIDDLE | BOTTOM]

FORM ELEMENTS

Tag	Description	Attributes
<FORM>...</FORM>	Input form. For defining an area on the page to contain objects for input from the reader	ACTION=url METHOD=[GET | POST]

Tag	Description	Attributes
<INPUT>	Defines an input object in a form	TYPE=[TEXT | CHECKBOX | RADIO | SUBMIT | RESET | HIDDEN] NAME=name VALUE=text SIZE=nchars MAXLENGTH=nchars CHECKED
<OPTION>...</OPTION>	Defines an item for a SELECT input object	SELECTED
<SELECT>...</SELECT>	Selection input object, popup menu	NAME=name SIZE=number MULTIPLE
<TEXTAREA>...</TEXTAREA>	Multiline input object	NAME=name ROWS=number COLS=nchars

HYPERTEXT LINKS

Tag	Description	Attributes
<A>...</A>	Anchor. Marks the start (HREF) or end (NAME) of a link	HREF=url NAME=name TITLE=text
<MAP>...</MAP>	Provides links for Client-side image-maps (N,3)	NAME=name
<AREA>	Defines an area within an imagemap (N,3)	COORDS=x,y,x,y SHAPE=[rect | polygon | circle] HREF=url NOHREF

INLINE IMAGES

Tag	Description	Attributes
<IMG>	Image. Used to place an inline image into the page	SRC=url ALT=text ISMAP ALIGN=[TOP | MIDDLE | BOTTOM] ALIGN=[LEFT | RIGHT] BORDER=pixels HEIGHT=pixels WIDTH=pixels HSPACE=pixels VSPACE=pixels USEMAP
<FIGURE>...</FIGURE>	Places a figure in the text (3)	SRC=url
<CAPTION>...</CAPTION>	Provides a caption for a figure (3)	ALIGN=[TOP | MIDDLE | BOTTOM]
<CREDIT>...</CREDIT>	Provides a credit line for a figure (3)	

PAGE MARKUP

Tag	Description	Attributes
<BASE>	Base. Provides a reference to resolve relative addressing	HREF=url
<BODY>...</BODY>	Designates the content of an HTML document	BGCOLOR=color BACKGROUND=url TEXT=color LINK=color ALINK=color VLINK=color
<HEAD>...</HEAD>	Head. Defines that part of the document containing information about the page	

Tag	Description	Attributes
<HTML>...</HTML>	Defines the extent of an HTML document	
<ISINDEX>	Indicates that a searchable index for the document is available on the server	
<LINK>	Provides information relating the current document to other documents or entities	HREF=url TITLE=text REL=server REV=server
<META>	Sends an http command to the server	HTTP-EQUIV=server CONTENT=number; url
<TITLE>...</TITLE>	Document title. Must be in document head	

Character Entities

Unlike markup tag and attribute names, character entities are case sensitive.

MARKUP ENTITIES

Definition	How It Appears	Entity
less than	<	<
greater than	>	>
ampersand	&	&
quote	"	"
copyright	©	©
registered	®	®
nonbreaking space		
any ASCII	§	§

LATIN 1 CHARACTERS

Definition	How It Appears	Entity
Uppercase AE diphthong (ligature)	Æ	&AElig;
Uppercase A, acute accent	Á	&Aacute;
Uppercase A, circumflex accent	Â	&Acirc;
Uppercase A, grave accent	À	&Agrave;
Uppercase A, ring	Å	&Aring;
Uppercase A, tilde	Ã	&Atilde;
Uppercase A, dieresis or umlaut mark	Ä	&Atilde;
Uppercase C, cedilla	Ç	&Ccedil;
Uppercase E, acute accent	É	&Eacute;
Uppercase E, circumflex accent	Ê	&Ecirc;
Uppercase E, grave accent	È	&Egrave;
Uppercase E, dieresis or umlaut mark	Ë	&Euml;
Uppercase I, acute accent	Í	&Iacute;
Uppercase I, circumflex accent	Î	&Icirc;
Uppercase I, grave accent	Ì	&Igrave;
Uppercase I, dieresis or umlaut mark	Ï	&Iuml;
Uppercase N, tilde	Ñ	&Ntilde;
Uppercase O, acute accent	Ó	&Oacute;
Uppercase O, circumflex accent	Ô	&Ocirc;
Uppercase O, grave accent	Ò	&Ograve;
Uppercase O, slash	Ø	&Oslash;
Uppercase O, tilde	Õ	&Otilde;
Uppercase O, dieresis or umlaut mark	Ö	&Ouml;
Uppercase U, acute accent	Ú	&Uacute;
Uppercase U, circumflex accent	Û	&Ucirc;
Uppercase U, grave accent	Ù	&Ugrave;

Definition	How It Appears	Entity
Uppercase U, dieresis or umlaut mark	Ü	&Uuml;
Uppercase Y, acute accent	Ý	&Yacute;
Lowercase a, acute accent	á	&aacute;
Lowercase a, circumflex accent	â	&acirc;
Lowercase ae diphthong (ligature)	æ	&aelig;
Lowercase a, grave accent	à	&agrave;
Lowercase a, ring	å	&aring;
Lowercase a, tilde	ã	&atilde;
Lowercase a, dieresis or umlaut mark	ä	&auml;
Lowercase c, cedilla	ç	&ccedil;
Lowercase e, acute accent	é	&eacute;
Lowercase e, circumflex accent	ê	&ecirc;
Lowercase e, grave accent	è	&egrave;
Lowercase e, dieresis or umlaut mark	ë	&euml;
Lowercase i, acute accent	í	&iacute;
Lowercase i, circumflex accent	î	&icirc;
Lowercase i, grave accent	ì	&igrave;
Lowercase i, dieresis or umlaut mark	ï	&iuml;
Lowercase n, tilde	ñ	&ntilde;
Lowercase o, acute accent	ó	&oacute;
Lowercase o, circumflex accent	ô	&ocirc;
Lowercase o, grave accent	ò	&ograve;
Lowercase o, slash	ø	&oslash;
Lowercase o, tilde	õ	&otilde;
Lowercase o, dieresis or umlaut mark	ö	&ouml;
Lowercase sharp s, German, (commonly substituted for the sz ligature)	ß	&szlig;

Definition	How It Appears	Entity
Lowercase u, acute accent	ú	&uacute;
Lowercase u, circumflex accent	û	&ucirc;
Lowercase u, grave accent	ù	&ugrave;
Lowercase u, dieresis or umlaut mark	ü	&uuml;
Lowercase y, acute accent	ý	&yacute;
Lowercase y, dieresis or umlaut mark	ÿ	&yuml;

Appendix B: Resources

General Guides to Cyberspace

Yahoo
http://www.yahoo.com/

The Clearinghouse for Subject-Oriented Internet Resource Guides
http://www.lib.umich.edu/chhome.html

The Guide to Network Resource Tools
http://www.earn.net/gnrt/notice.html

The Virtual Library: Subject Catalogue
http://www.w3.org/hypertext/DataSources/bySubject/Overview.html

A Guide to Cyberspace
http://www.hcc.hawaii.edu/guide/www.guide.html

Internet Resources Meta-Index
http://www.ncsa.uiuc.edu/SDG/Software/Mosaic/MetaIndex.html

InterNIC Directory Services
http://www.internic.net/

The Awesome List
http://www.clark.net/pub/journalism/awesome.html

Oneworld Directory
http://oneworld.wa.com/

The Learned InfoNet
http://info.learned.co.uk/

Charm Net Home Page
http://www.charm.net/

Planet Earth Home Page
http://white.nosc.mil/www.html

THE WORLD WIDE WEB

World Wide Web Home Page
http://www.w3.org/

World Wide Web Servers
http://www.w3.org/hypertext/DataSources/WWW/Geographical.html

World Wide Web FAQ
http://sunsite.unc.edu/boutell/faq/www_faq.html

Entering the World-Wide Web: A Guide to Cyberspace
http://www.eit.com/web/www.guide/

Technical Aspects of the World-Wide Web
http://www.w3.org/hypertext/WWW/Technical.html

WWW SEARCH SERVICES

WWW Search Engines
http://pubweb.nexor.co.uk/public/cusi/cusi.html

The Lycos Searching Engine
http://lycos.cs.cmu.edu/

Search WWW Space
http://riskweb.bus.utexas.edu/search.html

The WORLD WIDE WEB WORM
http://www.cs.colorado.edu/home/mcbryan/WWWW.html

HTML

Introduction to HTML
http://www.cwru.edu/help/introHTML/toc.html

A Beginner's Guide to HTML
http://www.ncsa.uiuc.edu/General/Internet/WWW/HTMLPrimer.html

HyperText Mark-up Language
http://www.w3.org/hypertext/WWW/MarkUp/MarkUp.html

Style Guide for Online Hypertext
http://www.w3.org/hypertext/WWW/Provider/Style/Overview.html

HTML Design Guide
http://ncdesign.kyushu-id.ac.jp/howto/text/Normal/html_design.html

MacMillan HTML Workshop
http://www.mcp.com/general/workshop

HTML: Working and Background Materials
http://www.w3.org/hypertext/WWW/MarkUp/MarkUp.html

HTML Specification Review Materials
http://www.w3.org/hypertext/WWW/ MarkUp/MarkUp.html

HTML Design Notebook
http://www.w3.org/hypertext/WWW/People/Connolly/drafts/
html-design.html

Netscape's Extensions to HTML
http://home.mcom.com/home/services_docs/html-extensions.html

A Quick Review of HTML 3.0
http://www.w3.org/hypertext/WWW/Arena/tour/start.html

HTML 3.0 Draft
http://www.hpl.hp.co.uk/people/dsr/html3/CoverPage.html

HTML 3.0 Test Pages
http://www.to.icl.fi/~aj/test_doc.html

WEB DEVELOPMENT

WWW Developer's Resources
http://www.uwtc.washington.edu/Computing/WWW/General.html

The WWW Developer's Virtual Library
http://WWW.Stars.com/

Archive of HTML Translators
ftp://src.doc.ic.ac.uk/computing/information-systems/www/tools/translators/

HTML Tools Library
http://www.awa.com/nct/software/webtools.html

The Common Gateway Interface: FORMS
http://hoohoo.ncsa.uiuc.edu/cgi/forms.html

HTML & CGI Unleashed
http://www.rpi.edu/~decemj/works/wdg.html

Introduction to Webscaping Documentation
http://www.utirc.utoronto.ca/HTMLdocs/NewHTML/intro.html

Netscape's How to Create Web Services
http://home.netscape.com/home/how-to-create-web-services.html

Cool Tricks: Homepage Development Tools
http://home.netscape.com/MCOM/tricks_docs/tools_docs/index.html

SINGNET HTML Developer's Jumpstation
http://www.singnet.com.sg/public/dev-page.html

WWW Software Products
http://www.w3.org/hypertext/WWW/Status.html

CERN's Tools for WWW Providers
http://www.w3.org/hypertext/WWW/Tools/

NASA's Tools for Web Weavers
http://www.nas.nasa.gov/NAS/Links/

Hypermedia Authoring Tools
http://info.mcc.ac.uk/CGU/staff/lilley/authoring.html

Internet Tools Summary
http://www.rpi.edu/Internet/Guides/decemj/itools/internet-tools.html

The Server Guide
http://www.w3.org/hypertext/WWW/Daemon/User/Guide.html

How to Create a WWW Server (A WWW FAQ)
http://www.w3.org/hypertext/WWW/FAQ/Server.html

World-Wide Web Proxies
http://www.w3.org/hypertext/WWW/Proxies/

The Common Gateway Interface
http://hoohoo.ncsa.uiuc.edu/cgi/overview.html

A CGI Programmer's Reference
http://www.best.com/~hedlund/cgi-faq/

Mosaic 2.0 Fill-Out Form Support
http://www.ncsa.uiuc.edu/SDG/Software/Mosaic/Docs/fill-out-forms/
overview.html

Check Your HTML with WEBlint
http://www.unipress.com/weblint/

HaLsoft HTML Validation
http://www.hal.com/~markg/WebTechs/validation-form.html

GOPHERS

Gopher
gopher://gopher.tc.umn.edu/11/Information About Gopher

Search Titles in Gopherspace Using veronica
gopher://gopher.tc.umn.edu:70/1/Other Gopher and Information
Servers/Veronica

Internet Resources
gopher://quest.arc.nasa.gov:70/1/resources

INDEX